DISCARD

—PEOPLE TO KNOW—

ELIE WIESEL

Voice From the Holocaust

Michael A. Schuman

ENSLOW PUBLISHERS, INC.

Bloy St. and Ramsey Ave.	P.O. Box 38
Box 777	Aldershot
Hillside, N.J. 07205	Hants GU12 6BP
U.S.A.	U.K.

To the six million and all other victims of oppression.

Library of Congress Cataloging-in-Publication Data

Schuman, Michael.
    Elie Wiesel: voice from the Holocaust / Michael A. Schuman.
       p. cm. — (People to know)
    Includes bibliographical references and index.
    ISBN 0–89490–428–0
    1. Wiesel, Elie, 1928- —Biography—Juvenile literature.
    2. Authors, French—20th century—Biography—Juvenile literature.
    3. Holocaust survivors—Biography—Juvenile literature. 4. Jewish
    authors—Biography—Juvenile literature. [1. Wiesel, Elie, 1928- .
    2. Holocaust, Jewish (1939–1945) 3. Authors, French.]
    I. Title. II. Series.
    PQ2683.I32Z87 1994
    813'.54—dc20
    [B]
                              93–27451
                                 CIP
                                 AC

Printed in the United States of America

10 9 8 7 6 5 4 3 2

Illustration Credits:
Boston University Photo Service, pp. 82, 101; David Valdez, White House,
p. 110; Dollos Memorial Holocaust Studies/Courtesy of United States
Holocaust Memorial Museum, p. 48; Franklin D. Roosevelt Library, pp.
28, 31; From the Archives of the Simon Wiesenthal Center, p. 92; From
the film *Sighet, Sighet,* Courtesy of Biograph Entertainment, pp. 15, 39;
Israel Ministry of Tourism, p. 90; Jimmy Carter Library, pp. 86, 88;
Michael A. Schuman, p. 6; National Archives/Courtesy of United States
Holocaust Memorial Museum, p. 50; Ronald Reagan Library, pp. 94, 97;
U.S. Army Military History Institute, pp. 43, 64; Courtesy of United States
Holocaust Memorial Museum, p. 113; YIVO Center for Jewish
Research/Courtesy of United States Holocaust Memorial Museum, p. 17.

Cover Illustration:
Michael A. Schuman

Contents

Acknowledgements

There were many persons and sources who were of extraordinary help in writing this book. However, two stand out.

One is the staff at the Holocaust Resource Center at Keene State College, Keene, New Hampshire. Dr. Charles A. Hildebrandt and Michelle J. Nash are doing a wonderful job at the center and they and their students' time and efforts are greatly appreciated.

The other is Professor Wiesel's office at Boston University. Professor Wiesel was especially gracious in lending me some time in his busy schedule and his assistant, Martha Hauptman, provided invaluable help. Professor Wiesel's teaching assistants, Janet McCabe and Joe Kanofsky, kindly permitted me to take advantage of their years of experience in knowing Elie Wiesel.

Elie Wiesel

1

Nobel Laureate

The people in the audience, all distinguished men and women, listened intently to every word spoken by the shy, sad-eyed man standing at the podium. Except for the clicking of camera shutters, there was hardly a sound from those gathered in the ceremonial hall at the University of Oslo in Norway. They paid rapt attention to the speaker, who was talking of his experience of both horrors and honors as he accepted the greatest award of his life.

The lecturer was Elie Wiesel and he was receiving the Nobel Peace Prize for 1986. Nobel Prizes pay tribute each year to men and women whose achievements have affected citizens all over the world. Nobel Prizes are awarded in the sciences, literature, and economics, but the Nobel Peace Prize could be the most highly regarded of them all. Wiesel was chosen for his work as a writer, teacher, philosopher, and advocate of peace.

There was a time in Wiesel's life when it looked as if he would never live to become an adult, let alone win such special recognition. Wiesel grew up in a village in Rumania in eastern Europe with his parents and three sisters in the 1930s. In 1939, World War II broke out, and their lives were changed forever.

Most young people at age fifteen spend their time attending school, playing sports, or falling in love for the first time. But when Elie was fifteen he and his family were taken from their home by police serving the German Nazis who had occupied Rumania. Under Adolf Hitler, who had established what was likely the most brutal dictatorship in this century, the Nazis had embarked on a course of evil that included killing all Jewish people as well as many others they considered inferior to themselves.

The Nazis had conquered almost all of Europe and in each of the countries they occupied, they captured Jews who were living peacefully in towns or villages and sent them to concentration camps, confined areas like prisons where they had to work as slaves. Many of the Jews were tortured and most were later put to death at separate death camps, which were built specifically for killing Jews and other "undesirables" like Gypsies. In many cases, the death camps were on the grounds of the larger concentration camps.

The Wiesel family was first sent to Auschwitz, a concentration camp in Poland, where his youngest sister and his mother were killed in gas chambers, small rooms filled with poisonous gas. His two older sisters were separated from the family and taken elsewhere. Meanwhile, Wiesel and his father were transported to a concentration camp in Germany called Buchenwald, where his father died from hunger and disease. It was only after the U.S. Army liberated Buchenwald three months later, that Wiesel, then sixteen, was rescued.

As an adult, Wiesel used the memories of his terrifying teenage years to try to ensure that such a catastrophe would never happen again. He did so by writing books and teaching at colleges about his experiences, warning that this type of terror could be repeated if bad dictatorships were not challenged, and advocating fair treatment for all oppressed peoples of the world. A religious man, Wiesel has spent his life urging people to reject bigotry, hatred, and violence.

In fact, Wiesel is given credit as one of the first people to use the term "Holocaust" to describe the Nazi mass killings, a word that is accepted by most people as the official label for those murders.[1]

As he gave his acceptance speech in Oslo, Wiesel brought his fourteen-year-old son up to the podium, to demonstrate the fact that despite years of oppression Jews continued to survive.

But he also recalled his experiences as a boy living in

concentration camps forty-one years earlier, and spoke in grief-stricken tones of his adolescence. He described himself in the third person, as if he was speaking about an entirely separate individual.

The fifty-eight-year-old Wiesel said:

> It happened yesterday or eternities ago, a young Jewish boy discovered the kingdom of the night. I remembered his bewilderment, I remember his anguish. It all happened so fast. The decrees. The deportation. The sealed cattle car. The fiery altar upon which the history of our people and the future of mankind were meant to be sacrificed.
>
> I remember: he asked his father: can this be true? This is the 20th century, not the Middle Ages. Who would allow such crimes to be committed? How could the world remain silent?
>
> And now the boy is turning to me: 'Tell me,' he asks. 'What have you done with my future? What have you done with your life?'
>
> And I tell him that I have tried. That I have tried to keep memory alive, that I have tried to fight those who would forget it. Because if we forget, we are guilty, we are accomplices.
>
> And then I explained to him how naive we were, that the world *did* know and remained silent. And that is why I swore never to be silent whenever and wherever human beings endure suffering and humiliation. We must always take sides. Neutrality helps the oppressor, never the victim. Silence encourages the tormentor, never the tormented."[2]

There was a bit of irony in the awarding of Wiesel's

1986 prize. Exactly fifty years earlier, the Nobel Peace Prize was given to a German pacifist named Carl von Ossietzky, who had tried to warn the people of his country about the growing strength of the Nazi party and the menace to peace it represented. Many at the time, even those who were moderates, denounced the honoring of Ossietzky with the prize as being an insult to the German government. Wiesel's message about speaking out and challenging evil leaders seemed even more poignant with that anniversary in mind.

At the end of his speech, Wiesel thanked the Norwegians, who responded by applauding in gratitude. As he left the auditorium and walked out into the cold Oslo afternoon, people on the street applauded him, too. Smiling, Wiesel turned to his family and friends and hugged them, realizing that his survival had meaning for humankind.[3]

2

A Studious Boy

Eliezer Wiesel grew up in a time and a place that have long since vanished. In Elie's world young people devoted their time mainly to two things: learning and more learning. The place was a village called Sighet in a region called Transylvania.

Most Americans today know Transylvania only as the home of the fictional vampire, Count Dracula. But Transylvania is a real place. It is an area in eastern Europe surrounded by the Carpathian Mountains. At different times in history Transylvania has been part of both Hungary and Rumania, although when Elie was born it was part of Rumania.

Eliezer, known in his family by the nickname Leizer, lived in a little house made of wood on a cobblestoned street in the Jewish section of Sighet. Most Jews of

Sighet, including Leizer—who would call himself Elie as an adult—were Hasidic Jews. They believe in the basic tenets of the Jewish religion, but give them their own special interpretation.

Jews believe in one all-powerful God, but, unlike Christians, Jews believe the Messiah has yet to come. Jews celebrate the Sabbath each week from sunset on Friday to sunset on Saturday. The Sabbath signifies the end of the work week, a time for rest and peacefulness. The Jewish religion celebrates many holidays throughout the year, the most important being Rosh Hashanah, or the Jewish New Year, which usually falls in September or early October, and Yom Kippur, the Day of Atonement, which comes ten days later. Another important holiday is Pesach, or Passover, which lasts eight days in the spring. It commemorates the exodus of the Jews out of ancient Egypt about 3,250 years ago.

Hasidic Jews, a small percentage of the total Jewish population, follow the writings and teachings of a man called the Baal Shem Tov, who lived in Poland in the mid-1700s. Many Hasidic Jews dress a certain way, with long beards and curled ringlets of hair by their ears. More importantly, they believe in a more mystical form of Judaism than do non-Hasidic Jews, and worship God through intense song and dance.

Jews have traditionally placed a strong emphasis on education and Elie, like most of the boys in his community, spent most of his time learning, either in school or on his own. If children had any time left over, they would spend it on leisure activities. But even then, Elie spent hardly any moments at play.

Elie recalls, "I didn't play much. Other youngsters I knew played football (soccer in the United States) or went bicycling. But I only played chess. It was the only thing I knew. I wasn't sports-oriented."[1]

It was common for Elie to spend his time alone. He had three sisters, two older and one seven years younger. But because of their age span they had different interests from Elie. And Elie was just as happy to stay indoors and read serious texts as to play outside.[2]

Like most of the other Jewish boys growing up in Sighet, Elie's main passion was acquiring knowledge. He first went to school at age three, but he was lonely being away from his family during the day. When he was a little older, Elie had a teacher who was known as Zeide the Melamed ("grandfather, the teacher"), but he was a grouchy man with a short temper who thought nothing of handing out corporal punishment when a student came to class late.

Elie especially enjoyed learning from his family, who spent a great deal of their time passing on their knowledge to him.[3] His mother, Sarah, taught by example. The Wiesel family was poor, as were most Jews in Sighet. But like most of her Jewish neighbors, Sarah managed to light candles every Sabbath, a Jewish custom, and she always offered the sacred blessings

Elie Wiesel as a young boy. Here, he is shown with (from left to right) his sister Beatrice, mother Sarah, and sister Hilda.

accompanying the lighting. Two of the family's most precious possessions were the silver candlesticks that held the Sabbath candles during the ceremony.

Yet Sarah was also an educated woman, one of the few in her day who had graduated from high school, and a very religious one, too. She passed on her faith to Elie, recommending that he learn the Torah, the Talmud (writings that form the basis of Jewish law and lore), and the beliefs of Hasidism. Elie remembered his mother's advice and teachings and appreciated them for the rest of his life.

Elie's father, Shlomo, was a shopkeeper, who owned and operated what would today be known as a general store. He observed the Sabbath and prayed regularly in the nearby synagogue (a Jewish house of worship), but Shlomo was not as faith-driven as Sarah. He instilled humanistic values in Elie, values that related to cooperation with and trust in other human beings. Though Shlomo was constantly busy with his store, he did make time, especially on the Sabbath, to teach his son more secular subjects, like history, literature, and modern Hebrew.

Elie had special feelings for his grandfather, a spirited and lively man with a long white beard, who was respected among the Hasidic Jews as an authority on their religion.[4] Known as Dodye Feig ("Little David"), Elie's grandfather owned a farm a few miles away, and in this time and place where most people didn't have

A group of yeshiva students in a weaving class in Sighet. This photo was taken during the time of Wiesel's youth.

automobiles, the trip from grandfather's farm to Elie's home was more than just a short jaunt.

Elie loved those special times when Dodye Feig traveled by horse and cart to visit, and he adored his grandfather's Hasidic stories and songs. Dodye Feig was Elie's best friend and confidant. Once the boy even ran away and roamed through the countryside until he reached his grandfather's place. Elie said he wasn't angry with his parents, he just missed his grandfather.

In a book he would write as a middle-aged adult called *A Jew Today,* Elie recalled how others thought warmly of his grandfather:

> People also loved him for his kindness. He gave freely of himself. No one ever left him empty-handed. . . . Dodye Feig was loved because of his passion for life, for people, trees, books, encounters. He illuminated souls by his mere presence.
>
> I remember him as a robust man, full of verve, always on the go; his cheeks were ruddy and wrinkled; his beard as white as snow; his voice warm and vibrant. . . .
>
> Whenever I felt sad or guilty or misunderstood, I would seek refuge with him. I would go and knock at his door or simply imagine him standing before me: 'Are you unhappy, little one? Do you have complaints against life? But then, what are you waiting for to change it? Come, I shall help you. Have I ever told you the marvelous theory of. . ." Yes or no, it made no difference; the small schoolboy forgot his sorrow.[5]

For a while in 1940, Elie's father, Shlomo, was absent from home. But this was through no will of his own. World War II was raging in Europe and Shlomo was secretly helping Jews escape from Nazi-occupied Poland. Shlomo was arrested by the authorities and jailed for two months, but then he was released and allowed to return home. He went back to his normal routine, and continued to assist escaped Jews. He spoke little of his prison experience.

About that time, when Elie was twelve years old, his appetite for basic religious studies had been satisfied and he wanted to enter more adult worlds of spirituality. It might be difficult for young people today to understand, but in Elie's small Jewish community religion and education were the keystones of daily life, even for children, and Elie was an especially studious youngster. It's hard to say how he would have been different if he had grown up in the secular world of today, where television, movies, and video games are diversions for many young people.

Elie was looking for answers to questions that most intelligent philosophers and scientists haven't been able to answer—questions like: When will there be permanent peace in the world? and What is the reason why human beings exist? He was hoping to study the *cabala*, a Jewish school of mystical thought, where every passage and verse in the Bible is interpreted with hidden meanings. Elie thought that here he might find the answers to his haunting questions about life.

In addition, Elie began fasting twice a week. He says today, "It was part of a religious period I went through. One of the things we used to do was fast Monday and Thursday. According to some religious discipline, it's good for your soul."[6]

Shlomo Wiesel thought his son was too young to learn the mysteries of the *cabala*, but Elie found his own teacher in a local man named Moshe, a poor, sad-eyed fellow who worked at the synagogue where Elie worshiped. He relished the sessions with Moshe and felt that Moshe accepted him not as a curious boy but as an adult.[7]

Later that year, Elie celebrated his bar mitzvah, a Jewish ceremony that takes place at age thirteen, marking the transition from boyhood to manhood. This is usually a very special and happy occasion for Jews. But the year of Elie's bar mitzvah was 1941, far from a happy time throughout Nazi-occupied Europe. Stories of the persecution and murder of Jews were reaching Sighet with alarming frequency. Gentile (non-Jewish) children in Sighet were picking on and fighting with Jewish youngsters for no other reason than the fact that they were Jewish. And in Elie's own family, there was the recent memory of Shlomo's months in jail.

With the family's safety in mind, Sarah seriously considered leaving Sighet for Palestine, the land that would eventually become Israel, which was seen as a haven for oppressed Jews. But Shlomo, an optimist who looked for the good in people, felt such a move was not necessary.[8]

It was common, he said, for Jews to suffer persecution from Gentiles at certain periods in history, and he felt confident that, as it had before, in time such persecution would end.[9]

3

World War II—The World in Turmoil

World War II didn't start overnight. Seeds of the war were planted as soon as World War I ended. Some Germans blamed the Jews for their country's defeat and as a result of this bigotry, in 1920, a tiny political party called the National Socialist German Workers Party, soon to be known by its German initials as the Nazi party, formed with sixty members. The Nazis believed in the opposite of democracy—that one party and, in particular, one man should lead their country.

Their creed was both nationalistic and racist. They proclaimed that only those of German blood could be members of their nation. They glorified racial superiority and felt that all Jews who had come to Germany after 1914, the year when World War I began in Europe, should be forced to leave.

In truth, German Jews had served proudly alongside German Christians during the battles of World War I, fighting in the trenches as citizens of their country in the same way that Jewish citizens of Britain and the United States fought for their homelands. More than 100,000 German Jews served in the German army. In fact, the first member of the German parliament to be killed in action was a Jewish man, Dr. Ludwig Haas. Following the war Jews played a major role in rebuilding their country and some of them held important government posts.

The Nazi party remained a minor one until the late 1920s when the economy in Germany was starting to sour. Inflation and unemployment were both rising sharply and by the end of 1929 more than three million Germans were out of work. Again, the Nazis said that the Jews were to blame for Germany's problems, and on New Year's Day 1930, eight innocent Jews were murdered in Berlin by storm troopers, armed thugs working for Nazi leader Adolf Hitler.

Similar Nazi attacks continued, as did verbal accusations directed at both Jews and the Nazis' political opponents. With the German economy suffering greatly, the Nazi party was in a position to gain power. The Nazis had held only 12 seats in the German parliament, or *Reichstag,* but in an election held on October 14, 1930, they gained an astounding 95 seats, to hold a total of 107.

With increased power, the Nazis felt free to step up their physical attacks on Jews, many of them elderly and defenseless. Still, the most visible concern for most of the German people was not this flagrant bigotry, but the possibility of being unemployed. Both the Communists on the far left and the Nazis on the far right courted votes from disenchanted Germans and in an election in June 1932 the Nazis under Hitler proved fairly successful.

The incumbent president, Field Marshal Paul von Hindenburg, was reelected, receiving 53 percent of the vote. But Hitler won 36 percent and the Communist candidate obtained only about 10 percent.

There were two more elections later that year, and after the second one in November, Hitler appeared to be losing power. But there was no clear winner, as is sometimes the case in elections that are part of a parliamentary system, and a compromise agreement was reached. Following that agreement, Hitler was named chancellor on January 30, 1933.

Almost immediately Hitler's regime began cracking down on Jews and opposition members. Jewish-owned stores were looted, Jewish attorneys and judges were banned from practicing, and Jewish businesses were boycotted. Many innocent Jews were beaten on the streets. And in a village called Dachau in the rolling countryside near Munich in southern Germany the first concentration camp was built. Here critics of Hitler's government were taken from their homes and gathered, or "concentrated" in camps behind barbed wire where they were forced to live.

In addition to blaming Jews for Germany's economic problems, the Nazis claimed that Jews were an inferior race to Germans. And in September of 1935 Hitler made this lie into law. The Nuremberg laws, as they came to be known, claimed that only those of German, or Aryan, blood could become citizens of Germany and that Jews were absolutely *not* of German blood. Jews were prohibited from displaying the German flag and marriages between Jews and Gentile Germans were outlawed.

The Nazi definition of "Jew" was broad. It meant not only practicing Jews, but also those who weren't religious. In this category the Nazis included people who were born Jewish who had later converted to Christianity and believed devoutly in Jesus, and even people whose parents had been born Jewish and had converted to Christianity.

Anti-Jewish feelings have a long history in Europe and some people in other countries agreed with the Germans. On the other hand, there were many observers in other countries who were outraged at the German actions but were preoccupied with their own problems. Tens of thousands of Jews were able to leave Germany, most of them to settle in Palestine. Many went to the United States, Great Britain, or other English-speaking countries that were then or had been part of the British Empire, such as Canada, Australia, and South Africa.

But there were limits to immigration laws in other countries, including the United States, and some Jews trying to emigrate were turned away. Thousands more made new homes in other parts of Europe, thinking they would be safe as long as they were outside Germany's borders. This would turn out not to be true. There were local citizens in other countries who aided Nazis by rounding up Jews, and anyway, in time the Nazis would control almost all of Europe.

The persecutions continued and more concentration camps were established over the next few years. Then in October 1938, an event occurred that would epitomize the beginning of the awful terror of the Holocaust. One of the many thousands of Jews evicted from their homes in Germany was a man named Zindel Grynszpan. He and others were sent to Poland on the grounds that they were Polish citizens. However, the Polish government refused to admit many of them, claiming that their Polish citizenship had expired. These deportees were crowded together in appalling conditions in a makeshift tent camp set up by the Polish army in a no-man's land along the Polish-German border.

Grynszpan's oldest son, Hirsch, was living in Paris. When he heard about his father's ordeal, he was so angry that he went to the German embassy and shot the first German official he saw.

Immediately, Hitler claimed the shooting was part of an international Jewish conspiracy to destroy Germany. When the official died, shortly afterward, the Nazis coordinated a massive outbreak of violence against Jews throughout Germany. Crowds tore through the streets, beating and killing Jews and destroying their homes. A total of 191 Jewish synagogues were looted and burned, and sacred prayer books and Torahs (treasured parchment scrolls containing the first five books of the Bible) were burned in the streets. The storm troopers then smashed the synagogue buildings and windows with axes and other tools.

During the outbreak, 91 Jews were killed and more than 30,000 were captured and sent to concentration camps. This night, November 9, 1938, would become known as *Kristallnacht*, which, literally translated means "night of broken glass."

Hitler, meanwhile, was not satisfied simply to destroy the Jewish people. His plan was to control Europe and much of what was then the Soviet Union. Some historians say that his ultimate plan was to control the world. In 1936, he signed pacts with the dictatorship in Italy and with Japan, and the three would be known during World War II as the Axis Powers. In March 1938, Hitler annexed Austria, and in September of that year he insisted that a part of Czechoslovakia called the Sudetenland, which contained a sizable number of

Adolf Hitler at the height of his power.

German-speaking people, actually *belonged* to Germany, and should be returned.

The leaders of France and Great Britain, desperate to prevent war from breaking out, signed an agreement with Hitler, giving Germany the Sudetenland if Hitler would respect the independence of the rest of Czechoslovakia. The treaty was signed and British Prime Minister Neville Chamberlain hailed it as "peace in our time." Most of the 20,000 Jews who lived in the Sudetenland fled to other parts of Czechoslovakia

Just six months later Hitler broke his promise and, on March 15, 1939, the German armies invaded and captured the rest of Czechoslovakia. Barely six months after that, on September 1, 1939, Germany invaded Poland. Within two days France and Britain responded by declaring war on Germany.

The following spring, German armies captured Denmark and invaded Norway before turning their attention to the Netherlands, Belgium, and France. By the end of 1940 the Nazis controlled nearly all of western Europe and had begun an aerial blitz on England. Separated from the continent of Europe by the English Channel, England had traditionally been considered safe from invading European armies. Air war changed that conception permanently—but Britain was saved by the fighter planes of the Royal Air Force in what is now known as the Battle of Britain.

The United States entered the war after Japan

bombed the U.S. Naval Base at Pearl Harbor in Hawaii on December 7, 1941. Prior to the Japanese attack, the American people had been split on whether or not the United States should be involved in the war in Europe. Now they were unified on the matter, realizing that if the Japanese could capture vital islands in the Pacific Ocean, the coast of California would be their next step. On December 8, President Franklin D. Roosevelt declared war. The opening words of his speech are now world-famous:

"Yesterday, December 7, 1941—a day which will live in infamy—the United States of America was suddenly and deliberately attacked by naval and air forces of the Empire of Japan."

On December 11, Germany declared war on the United States.

While the fighting in World War I was concentrated almost entirely in Europe, World War II was truly a case of the world at war. There were battles on or off the coasts of each of the six inhabited continents.

When the United States entered the war in late 1941, things looked bleak for the Allies. The Axis powers were in command in most of Europe, North Africa, and the Far East. It wasn't until 1943 that the tide started to turn and on June 6, 1944, the Allies conducted the largest invasion in the history of the world when more than 120,000 men landed on the beaches of Normandy in Nazi-occupied France. The Allies smashed through German defenses, liberating Normandy, the

U.S. President Franklin D. Roosevelt as he declared war against Japan on December 8, 1941. Several days later, Germany declared war on the United States.

French capital of Paris, and the little country of Luxembourg in just over three months.

By autumn 1944, the Axis powers were losing on all fronts and less than a year after the invasion of Normandy, on May 8, 1945, Germany surrendered. Italy had surrendered earlier and the war finally ended on September 2, 1945, when Japan signed an unconditional surrender aboard the U.S.S. *Missouri*. The dropping of two atom bombs, then a newly invented weapon of war, on Japan in early August hastened the Japanese surrender.

The casualties were staggering. Included among the estimated thirty million dead were more than six million Jewish civilians. While the war was being fought, Hitler accelerated his persecution of Jews in Germany and, as the Nazis conquered other countries, in those nations as well. The Nazis also slaughtered millions of others whom they hated, including Gypsies, Communists, homosexuals, and Jehovah's Witnesses. But their favorite targets were Jews.

More and more concentration camps, like the one at Dachau, were built. Some, known as death camps, changed from places of confinement to actual factories for killing people systematically. It was in these death camps that Jews were tortured and murdered in the cruelest ways. The majority of Nazis viewed Jews as less than human and in many cases treated them with appalling brutality.

Jewish children were terrorized and killed just as adults were. Some Jewish babies, screaming in fear, were thrown from windows as Nazis on the ground below tried to catch them on bayonets. There were times when lively, happy babies, too young to know what was happening around them, were taken from their mothers and beaten against walls until they died, then returned to their mothers' arms.[1]

Many Jews, especially women and twins, were the subjects of inhumane medical experiments. A common part of their treatment included slave labor where men, women, and children were deliberately humiliated. They were ordered to collect human waste or other refuse, for example. These tasks were completed on an empty stomach since those living in the camps were fed sparingly. Any who complained, fell out of line, or were just too weak to work were shot to death.

None was allowed to keep his or her private possessions and most were forced to strip naked in public. When clothed, they had to wear badges with a yellow Star of David, symbol of the Jewish religion. Ultimately, these Jews would be put to death by torture, shooting, or poisonous gas.

This was all part of the Nazis' goal to persecute and destroy the Jews of the world. They called it The Final Solution. This was the world that Elie Wiesel, at age fifteen entered in the spring of 1944.

4

Year of Horror[1]

Although the persecution of the Jews in Europe was in full swing in the early 1940s, many Jews were not aware of what was really happening. News of mass murders and Nazi plans to annihilate the Jewish people was being reported in the Jewish press, and in other newspapers in Europe and the United States, but many people, Jews and Gentiles alike, refused to believe it.

Some felt these tales of horror were just rumors, while many considered them typical wartime propaganda. Others believed such a massive plan was simply impossible, especially in the twentieth century. This type of brutality, they thought, happened only in the Dark Ages.

Most of the residents of Sighet were among those who refused to believe the stories were true. They even held onto these thoughts despite at least one eyewitness account.

In 1942, while Sighet and the region surrounding it formed part of Hungary, which was then an ally of Nazi Germany, all foreign-born Jews were forced to leave town. Wiesel's older friend Moshe, the humble and righteous man he studied the *cabala* with, was foreign-born and was taken away with hundreds of others on crowded railroad cars. Local Jews were upset and angry, but some thought that a deportation like this was not unusual in the middle of a war.

After several months Moshe returned to Sighet, telling horrible stories about the mass murders of people who had accompanied him on that train ride out of Sighet. He said that adult Jews were forced by the Gestapo (the Nazi security police) to dig their own graves, after which they were shot. Moshe told how babies were tossed into the air and used as targets by gun-toting Germans. He related the story of a young girl who was shot, then lay in agony for three days until she finally died. Moshe stated that the only reason *he* was alive was that he had only been wounded by the Gestapo's shots, but had lain in a pile of corpses pretending to be dead. When he knew the Gestapo were not around, he had managed to escape.

Nobody believed him. Nobody could imagine that such cruelty could take place in their day and age. As is typical of human nature, some people of Sighet thought terrible things like this only happened to others. They felt sure Moshe was exaggerating, trying to make people feel sorry for him. Others even thought he had gone insane.

Wiesel later admitted that he didn't believe Moshe's frightening stories either. And the people of Sighet went on with their normal routines: going to school, working at their jobs, falling in love, getting married, meeting with friends.

Even when the Nazis overran Hungary in 1944, and German tanks were rolling through the streets of Sighet, many people believed that the invaders would just be passive occupiers. Word had reached the residents of Sighet that the Jews of Budapest, the capital of Hungary, were being attacked by the Nazis. But, again, people felt it would not happen to them.

To Wiesel and the other residents of Sighet, the first appearances of the Germans were not frightening. The soldiers moved into private homes, including the home just across the street from the Wiesels, and they seemed to be pleasant guests. One soldier bought a box of candy for his hosts, the Kahn family, who were also neighbors of the Wiesels.

But this kindness was short-lived. On the seventh day of Passover the Nazis arrested all the Jewish leaders of Sighet. The remaining Jews were ordered to stay inside their homes for three days or be killed. Hungarian police invaded Jewish homes and demanded that the owners give up all their valuable belongings.

Shortly afterward, all Jews were forced to wear the dreaded yellow star, which indicated their religion to the Germans. Even at that point, Shlomo refused to admit he was scared—although the young son thought his father might have been frightened inside but didn't want to upset the family by showing his true feelings.

More restrictions were imposed upon the Jews. They were barred from riding trains, praying in their synagogues, and entering restaurants. Before too long, the Jewish neighborhood of Sighet was fenced in with barbed wire, becoming a small ghetto in a world unto itself.

Then the Jews' worst fears came true. The order for deportation was given and the Jews of Sighet were packed into unbearably crowded railroad cars and taken to an unknown destination. Those close to the windows, watching the scenery go by, realized they were being taken out of town. As the hours passed, it was apparent they were being transported out of Hungary altogether.

About midnight the train arrived at its final destination. An awful smell of burning flesh welcomed the terrified passengers to a place called Birkenau, a death camp on the grounds of the most notorious of the concentration camps: Auschwitz, west of the city of Krakow, in Poland.

Immediately, men and women were separated by an

SS officer holding a club. (The SS officers were in charge of Hitler's brutal death squads.) Wiesel watched his mother take the hand of his little sister, Tzipora, and with his two older sisters, walk away in the dark of the night. There was no way he could have known that he would never see his mother or baby sister again.

Young Wiesel, holding his father's hand, was forced to march with the other males, while SS officers called them swine, telling them they were about to be burned to death in huge ovens, or crematories, whose flames were plainly in view through the night air. Some younger Jews who were healthy and strong and carried knives talked about turning on their armed Nazi guards and attacking them, but the older Jews felt that would be foolish. They were outnumbered and could not win.

As the prisoners were led toward the crematories, Wiesel saw something he could not believe. A truck full of babies and little children pulled up to a ditch filled with a raging fire and dumped them into the flames. Wiesel felt this must all be part of a terrible nightmare; unfortunately, it was very real.

Wiesel, his father, and the others, in tears, were led closer and closer to the fire and Elie was certain he was about to be burned to death. When they were just two steps from the flames they were ordered to turn around and enter the barracks where they would be staying. Never, Wiesel said, would he forget the horrors of that

Elie Wiesel as a boy with his mother and little sister, Tzipora. When Wiesel saw them walk away in the darkness, he could not have known that he would never see them again.

night, and the faces of the babies and children burned alive.

The men were ordered to strip naked and run outdoors. They were disinfected and given prison clothes to wear. An SS officer appeared and gave them orders. They were to work as commanded or face death in the crematory.

Like all the prisoners, young Eliezer Wiesel was tattooed with a number, and from then on, he was known only by that number. It was as if he had no name. Wiesel was number A-7713. That's all. Number A-7713.

For weeks afterward Wiesel and his father were forced to live like slaves. They labored for long and brutal hours and were given only three sparse meals a day, just enough to survive: black coffee in the morning, soup at noon, and bread and margarine in the evening.

After their meager dinner, the men, in their cramped barracks, would talk, sometimes wondering out loud whether God existed and if so, why he would allow such brutality. Now and then the son and his father speculated about what had happened to Elie's mother and sisters. They would answer by reassuring each other that they were probably alive, working in some labor camp. But neither really believed it.

Months passed and Wiesel was transferred with his father to a factory called Buna, which was part of the concentration camp at Auschwitz. Again, they were put to work although the labor at first was not oppressive. Mostly, the Wiesels counted electrical fittings. Wiesel and his father were allowed to stay together in a barracks and soon Elie became friends with two young brothers from Czechoslovakia whose parents had been murdered at Birkenau.

The reality of life in a concentration camp was that torture and cruelty were always at hand. Once, a Nazi who was in control accused Wiesel's father of laziness and repeatedly beat him with an iron bar. All the teenager could do was stand by helplessly, since if he interfered he would have been beaten or killed. Another time, Elie was whipped twenty-five times on his bare back after he had unintentionally found a young Nazi guard alone with a girl.

On another occasion, the barracks foreman demanded to have a gold crown covering a tooth in Wiesel's mouth. This was common: the Nazis would melt down crowns taken from prisoners' teeth and keep the valuable gold. Wiesel refused to turn his crown over and in response the foreman mercilessly beat Shlomo, using the excuse that he was marching out of step. (The prisoners were always ordered to march in step when being taken anywhere as a group.)

Eventually, Wiesel gave in and said that the foreman could take his crown. The foreman responded that because he had been made to wait days for the crown, he would take Wiesel's daily ration of bread and give it to the dentist as a reward. The dentist removed the crown with a rusty spoon in the barracks bathroom.

A few days later, the foreman was sent to another camp. If he had waited a few more days, Wiesel would not have had to lose the crown and undergo the pain of its extraction. As he later said, he lost it for nothing.

When the Jewish High Holidays of Rosh Hashanah and Yom Kippur arrived, the normally religious young man found himself questioning and accusing God, rather than pleading for forgiveness for his sins, as is the practice. But the prisoners did manage to conduct a service within the confines of the barbaric concentration camp.

As the days grew shorter and the year came to a close, treatment of the prisoners became more and more vicious. Beatings were common and food rations grew smaller. Working outdoors in thin clothing in the biting winter cold, the men's health was getting increasingly worse.

A few weeks after the new year of 1945 began, Wiesel developed a swollen foot from exposure to the freezing temperatures. He was sent to the hospital, where he found conditions were far better than in the barracks. The food rations were larger and he did not have to work. Once in a while he could save up an extra piece of bread to give to his father.

A sick man lying next to him warned Wiesel to leave the hospital as soon as he could because the Germans

A group of starving prisoners at a concentration camp in Evansce, Austria. As at Buna, food rations were small, and clothing was very thin.

neither wanted nor needed sick or invalid Jews. Wiesel knew that the weakest Jews, those who could not work and therefore were of no use to the Nazis, were rounded up regularly and put to death. He had witnessed that process, called selection, many times with his own eyes.

The next morning a doctor operated on Wiesel's foot, draining the pus that was causing the swelling. Wiesel had feared that his leg might have to be amputated, but the doctor told him that he would be completely recovered in two weeks.

However, just two days later the rumor went through the camp that the Russian army, which was allied with the United States, was advancing on Buna. There had often been rumors about being rescued, but by that afternoon it was learned that this time the rumors were true and that all the prisoners were to be evacuated and sent to another camp.

Orders were to leave the hospital patients where they were and not evacuate them. Wiesel and the others with him thought this might mean they were to die, but they did not know exactly how. One patient predicted that the invalids and others in poor health would be gathered up and sent to the crematory to be burned to death. Another thought the camp would be blown up as soon as its evacuation was complete.

Wiesel was thinking more about his father than himself. Months of living with fear, brutality, and death all around him had made him—and many others—immune to fears about dying. So he fled the hospital, walking on his bare injured foot in the snow, to find his father and try to make a plan.

At one point the two considered trying to have Shlomo admitted as a patient so that he, too, could be in the hospital when the Russian army reached the camp, on the chance that they might be rescued. But that was too risky. They decided to evacuate with the rest of the healthy prisoners, even though Wiesel's foot was now bleeding openly.

They went back to the barracks for their last night at Buna, and they could hear the artillery of the Red Army in the distance. They had hoped the Russians would reach the camp before it was evacuated. But this was not to be. The next morning the prisoners were forced to march out of Buna in a blinding snowstorm, Elie hobbling along with his foot wrapped in a blanket.

After the war had ended, Wiesel learned what had happened to the patients who remained in the hospital. In spite of all their fears and worries, they were freed by the Russians with no harm coming to them.

For young Elie Wiesel and his father, the worst lay ahead. The death march went on for more than forty miles through appalling wintry conditions before the men were given time to rest. Those men who were weak, who couldn't endure, who lagged behind, were shot by the SS officers in command. Some sick men just fell to the ground and were trampled to death by the thousands of feet forced to continue marching. Nobody was allowed to stop to help another prisoner, whether it was his father, brother, or best friend, and none was permitted to stop even to catch his breath.

Wiesel later admitted that dying seemed to be the lesser of two evils, compared to the continued torture of that dreadful march, but he felt that for his father's sake he must stay alive. He knew nobody would take care of Shlomo if he died.

After they had marched through a deserted town, the SS finally gave an order to rest. Elie and his father found refuge with hundreds of other prisoners in the shell of a former brick factory building with a caved-in roof. Snow covered the floor and Wiesel fell asleep in the snow. It was the closest to a warm bed that he had slept on in what seemed like an eternity. His father slept a little, too. Men all around them were dying, and some prisoners, their bodies wracked by exhaustion, just fell asleep next to the dead men.

The prisoners were marched to another concentration camp called Gleiwitz, where they stayed for three days. At dawn on the third day they were driven out into the snow once more, to wait for a train that would take them to yet another camp. A small ration of bread was brought out and the men pounced upon it. Parched with thirst, they ate snow to feel the refreshing sensation of moisture running down their throats. The SS commanders laughed as if this was the funniest thing they had ever seen.

After waiting for hours the men were herded onto the train into open cattle cars. The train rolled on for some hours before stopping beside an open field. Here the bodies of those who had died along the way were thrown outside onto the ground.

Two men found Elie's father lying cold and still. The son rubbed his father's hands and slapped his face, desperately trying to wake him up. The men told Wiesel that his father was dead and he should let them toss him outside with the other corpses. Wiesel slapped his father fiercely and, finally, Shlomo's eyelids moved. He breathed slightly. Satisfied that Shlomo was alive, the two men went on, tossing other bodies outside.

For ten days the train moved on into the heart of Germany. The men were given no food and they survived by eating snow. By the time the train arrived at its destination, the concentration camp at Buchenwald, only about 100 men were able to climb out. The rest were either dead or were too weak to stand. Both Wiesel and his father were able to stand and leave.

But Shlomo Wiesel was a feeble, frail man. After a few days in Buchenwald he contracted dysentery, an illness of the digestive system which causes fever and diarrhea. He was not fed the usual sparse bread ration because the orders were not to waste food on those who were sick. A German doctor came, but he said his

Wiesel and his father, along with the other prisoners from Buna,
were moved to Buchenwald in early 1945. This photo shows the
camp soon after it was liberated later that year.

specialty was surgery and he could not help someone with dysentery. Another German doctor came, but he just humiliated the sick men, yelling at them and telling them they were lazy and only wanted to stay in bed. As Shlomo Wiesel called out for water and moaned in pain, a German officer beat him on the head with a stick, saying he was making too much noise.

Wiesel last saw his father when he went to bed on the night of January 28, 1945. When he awoke the next morning, another man was in his father's place. Shlomo Wiesel had been taken away to the crematory. Wiesel never knew whether his father was actually dead at the time.

Wiesel was taken to a block at Buchenwald that had been set up just for children. He was one of 600 kept there. Just over two months later, the Allies were approaching Buchenwald and the Germans started gradually evacuating the camp. On April 10, 1945, however, when about 20,000 prisoners remained, several hundred of whom were children, orders were given to evacuate the entire camp immediately. Suddenly, sirens wailed and the prisoners were forced back to their blocks, to be evacuated the next day.

The next morning the prisoners were gathered together once again. But the camp's underground resistance organization struck out against the Germans with grenades and guns. Within a couple of hours the SS

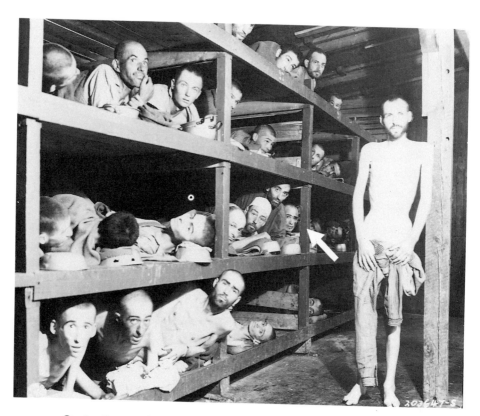

On April 11, 1945, Wiesel's camp was liberated. This photo shows Wiesel (white arrow), age sixteen, in his bunk amongst a sea of sick and starving prisoners.

men fled and the resistance group took over camp operations.

About six hours later American troops arrived to liberate the camp. A photograph was taken of Wiesel's bunk. It shows sixteen-year-old Elie Wiesel half submerged in a sea of sick and starving prisoners.

Three days later Wiesel was stricken with food poisoning. He spent the next two weeks in the hospital before being released. When he looked in the hospital mirror and saw himself for the first time since he had been taken prisoner, he said he looked like a corpse.

5

Vow of Silence

Elie Wiesel was alive and now free from the madness of
the Nazi death camps. But while his life had been saved,
it had also been turned inside out. Many thoughts went
through Wiesel's mind as he lay in his hospital bed.
Where do I go now? Should I go back to Sighet? But
with my parents dead and the Jewish community gone,
could it ever seem like home again? What do I do?[1]

Wiesel, at the young age of sixteen, was certain that
his whole family, including his three sisters, had been
killed. Lists of survivors that were published included
none of their names. With nowhere to go and no family
to find, Wiesel was gathered with 400 other children and
teenagers who had survived the camps and put on a train
heading out of Germany. The first plans were to send

them to Belgium where they would be placed in orphanages and cared for by social workers.

But when it was learned that Charles de Gaulle, the leader of the Free French during World War II and President of France in 1945, would accept the youngsters, the train headed for France. Many French castles were set aside by a group called the *Oeuvre de Secours aux Enfants,* or OSE (meaning "Children's Relief Work,") to house orphaned children until they could become assimilated into the French way of life. Wiesel lived in several of these big houses until early 1946, when he moved to Paris to earn his own way and live by himself.

Just after his arrival in France, while he was living with other refugee children in a castle in Normandy, Elie was given some surprising news. One day, the director of the home notified Wiesel that his older sister, Hilda, had just called on the telephone.

Wiesel didn't believe it.[2] He had never seen her name on lists of concentration camp survivors and he was certain she was among the millions that had been killed.

He took a train to Paris the next day and met Hilda at the train station. She said that she had recognized her brother in a photograph of a group of refugee children that was printed in her local newspaper. Immediately, she called the castle where the photo had been taken and asked to speak with her brother.

Both Hilda and Elie's older sister, Beatrice, had been held at the same concentration camp and both survived. In fact, Beatrice was now married to another camp survivor and living in a one-room apartment, too small to hold three. It was also impractical for Wiesel to move in with Hilda and her husband. Their space, too, was small and they were poor. After they talked it over, it made more sense for Wiesel to stay where he was where he would continue to be supported by the OSE.

Once he felt he could handle life on his own, Elie moved to Paris at age seventeen. His dream was to study at the Sorbonne, the capital's world-famous university. While he had always been fascinated by literature and philosophy, Wiesel's experience in the death camp and his year of horror had made him much more intrigued by man's relationship to his fellow man, and to the world around him.

How could such incredibly monstrous events occur, he wondered, and was there any meaning to this insanity? He felt it was important to tell the world of his experiences, in hopes that similar ones would never happen to someone else. Yet at this point in his life, Wiesel could not speak the language of his new country fluently. In addition, he was still trying to grasp the enormity of what had happened to him and the Jewish people of Europe. For both these reasons, he felt this was no time to try to tell his tale to the rest of the world.[3]

So in 1948 Wiesel enrolled at the Sorbonne. There

he attended lectures on topics such as philosophy, psychology, and literature, and was introduced to new ideas and new writers. In particular, he was impressed with French author Albert Camus, whose optimistic approach to human life and love for his fellow man inspired Wiesel, and warmed his own bitter feelings about life. He began to feel a will to live.

But people must pay to study and Wiesel, now on his own, no longer was aided by the OSE. To earn his keep, the young student took jobs tutoring children in Hebrew and the Talmud. At times Wiesel also worked as a summer camp counselor and choir director.

In May of 1948, Israel declared itself a nation. This fact was accepted by the United Nations, but not by Israel's Arab neighbors, who rejected the idea of a Jewish homeland in what had been the British mandate of Palestine. Elie wanted to go to Israel to help his country in its battle for independence, but because of his weakened condition, he was denied admission to the Israeli army.

Determined to find a way to Israel, Wiesel applied for jobs in journalism with the goal of covering the new nation's struggle to survive. He was hired by a French newspaper called *L'Arche*, then by an Israeli one, *Yediot Aharonot*, which needed a Paris correspondent. For the next several years while Wiesel was based in Paris, he accepted assignments that had him packing for destinations all over the world. These included Africa, South America, and India.

It was while on assignment in India in 1952 that the industrious reporter taught himself to speak English. At the same time, he began writing a dissertation comparing and contrasting the fundamentals and tenets of the Jewish, Christian, and Hindu religions, a lengthy work that he was never fully to complete.

One topic Wiesel did not write about, nor discuss, was his own experience in the Nazi concentration camps. He had taken a personal vow of silence, promising to himself not to publicly discuss anything regarding that frightening year. He couldn't find the words to describe to others all the feelings he had in response to those days of torture. In some ways Wiesel was unable to come to terms with the atrociousness of the Holocaust. His silence on the subject was to last a total of ten years.

By 1954, Wiesel was fully involved in his career as a journalist and still a full year away from ending his self-imposed silence concerning the Holocaust. One assignment from his employer, the Israeli newspaper *Yediot Aharonot*, led him to a meeting with the French author François Mauriac, who had won the Nobel Prize for literature in 1952.

Mauriac, a French Catholic, was a sensitive and religious man who had grown up in a very strict upper-middle-class home in the city of Bordeaux in southwestern France. His novels were known for being somber and stern, and they often were on the theme of man's struggle between the flesh and the spirit. In several works, Mauriac's characters embark on a search for love through human contact but can only find it through contact with God.

Mauriac also spoke out against political injustice. In the 1930s, when the seeds of World War II were being planted, he denounced totalitarianism, a form of government in which one person or group of people maintains absolute power over an entire country. At the same time he condemned the Fascist governments in Italy and Spain.

During the war, Mauriac was an active member of the French Resistance, those citizens of France who opposed the invading Germans and their ideology. He was an enthusiastic supporter of French General Charles de Gaulle, and went on to write a biography of the commander shortly before his death in 1970.

During the course of the meeting, Mauriac, well aware that Wiesel was representing an Israeli publication, praised the Jewish people and, specifically, Jesus, who was born Jewish. Mauriac said he viewed Jesus as a Jew who suffered and died to save all mankind.

Listening to Mauriac, Wiesel grew frustrated when his subject failed to mention the recent terrible history of the Jews. Wiesel finally said to Mauriac, "Ten years ago I knew hundreds of Jewish children who suffered more than Christ did. And no one talks about it."[4]

Mauriac was not immediately defensive, as many people might have been. Instead, he let the impact of Wiesel's words sink in. Then he began to cry. Mauriac conceded that the Christian world did indeed share responsibility for the atrocities of the Holocaust. He told his interviewer that if no one else has taken the first step to speak about the Holocaust, then *he* should be the one. That was the spur Wiesel needed.

Wiesel discounts the notion, accepted by some, that it was Mauriac who broke his vow of silence. Wiesel recalls, "When I met Mauriac it had been nine years since I entered that crazy world. I would have ended the vow of silence anyway. He simply helped me bring my words to a publisher. He was the catalyst."[5]

6

The Kingdom of the Night

A disciplined man, Wiesel began writing in Yiddish, his native language, recounting every detail of his life during the war. He began his story in 1941, three years before he entered the concentration camps, but a time when the war in Europe was already going at full blast and many Jews were being persecuted. He continued to write for an entire year, and when he lifted pen from paper for the final time his manuscript totaled 800 pages.

The huge volume of horror was titled in Yiddish, *Un di Velt Hot Geshvign*, which in English means, "And the World Remained Silent." Before long, Wiesel was able to get the book—all 800 pages—published in Argentina in Yiddish.

Publishing the book elsewhere wasn't so easy. Book publishers weren't interested in anything that large, so

Wiesel took time to drastically but carefully cut the book down to a shorter length. By the time he finished, the text had been trimmed to 127 pages. Wiesel then translated it into French, hoping to sell it in the country where he had settled. He also gave it a new title, *La Nuit*, which in English means, "Night."

Wiesel presented the book to François Mauriac, with whom he now had a sincere friendship. Mauriac agreed to write the foreword to the book, in which he recounted his first meeting with Wiesel:

> I confided to my young visitor that nothing I had seen during those somber years had left so deep a mark upon me as those trainloads of Jewish children standing at Austerlitz station. Yet I did not even see them myself! My wife described them to me, her voice still filled with horror. . . . This, then, was what I had to tell the young journalist. And when I said, with a sigh, "How often I've thought about those children!" he replied, "I was one of them."
>
> He had seen his mother, a beloved little sister, and all his family except for his father disappear into an oven fed with living creatures. As for his father, the child was forced to be a spectator day after day to his martyrdom, his agony, and his death. And such a death! The circumstances of it are related in this book, and I will leave the discovery of them and of the miracle by which the child himself escaped to his readers, who should be as numerous as those of *The Diary of Anne Frank*.[1]

Mauriac's words were to be prophetic. Wiesel's first

book has since become a classic, and while its readers may not have matched the numbers that have studied Anne Frank's world-famous diary, it has surely been read by millions.

But at the time Mauriac wrote those words, Elie Wiesel was still an unpublished young journalist. Mauriac put his efforts into helping the book to be published in France, which happened in 1958. The author dedicated the book to the memory of his parents and his little sister, Tzipora.

La Nuit was different from other books on the Holocaust that had been published in France up to that time in that it focused on one specific family—Wiesel's family—rather than on the entire event in general. There were also various subthemes, like the relationship between father and son, since much of the book follows Wiesel's imprisonment with his father in the concentration camps.

Another subtheme was man's relationship with God, and even whether or not God existed. Wiesel wrote the following in *La Nuit* about a fellow prisoner in the concentration camp:

> I knew a rabbi from a little town in Poland, a bent old man, whose lips were always trembling. He used to pray all the time, in the block, in the yard, in the ranks. He would recite whole pages of the Talmud from memory, argue with himself, ask himself questions and answer himself. And one day

he said to me: "It's the end. God is no longer with us."

And, as though he had repented of having spoken such words, so clipped, so cold, he added in his faint voice:

"I know. One has no right to say things like that. I know. Man is too small, too humble and inconsiderable to seek to understand the mysterious ways of God. But what can I do? I'm not a sage, one of the elect, nor a saint. I'm just an ordinary creature of flesh and blood. I've got eyes, too, and I can see what they're doing here. Where is the divine Mercy? Where is God? How can I believe, how could anyone believe, in this merciful God?"[2]

La Nuit became fairly successful in France, where it was both appreciated by critics and purchased by the public. And the book brought Elie Wiesel some renown.

In the United States, however, Wiesel and *La Nuit* were still unknown. Wiesel, who was now living in New York after being transferred there by *Yediot Aharonot,* tried with his agent to have *La Nuit* published in America. But in his adopted homeland he ran into repeated roadblocks.

Publishers were hesitant to take on this tale that depicted humankind at its worst. The most common opinion from publishers was that nobody would want to read a book that was so sad. Others simply didn't like the way the book read. One rejection, from Scribner's, a well-respected New York publisher, was representative. It read, "We have certain misgivings as to the size of the American market for what remains, despite Mauriac's brilliant introduction, a document."[3]

For a year Wiesel's agent pushed for publication of *La Nuit* and in the course of that time the book was turned down by dozens of publishers. Finally, in 1959, a company named Hill and Wang purchased the rights to publish *La Nuit* in the United States. The title was translated into English: *Night*, and the book was published in English in 1960.

But, as the publishers had warned, many people didn't want to hear about these tales of terror of the Holocaust—and they included large numbers of American Jews. The subject was just too depressing. *Night* sold just over 1,000 copies—a very small number for a title from a major publisher—in the first year and a half it was in the bookstores.

Gradually, that changed. In fact, some credit *Night* as the book that altered the attitudes of people in America about the Holocaust. Instead of hiding the horrible subject under the rug as many American Jews did for fifteen years after World War II ended, they began to discuss the Holocaust—its meaning and its cost, and ways to prevent another one from happening.

Since that initial hesitancy, *Night* has been studied and analyzed over and over again by historians, philosophers, teachers, and theologians—Christians as well as Jews.

American reporters view bodies at Buchenwald in 1945. At that time, many American Jews did not want to hear about the Holocaust. It was not until fifteen years later that they began to discuss the subject.

It isn't really surprising to many observers that a fellow Jewish writer, Cynthia Ozick, underlines the importance of *Night* when she said the book "brings us news from hell" and that Wiesel is "breaking through to a world blinded by its own fog."[4]

On the other hand, twenty-five years after *Night*'s first publication in the United States, George Will, a political columnist and analyst, who is a Christian, stressed that it is vital that *all* people read the book. In 1985, he said that reading *Night* was "perhaps the most effective way to introduce young people to a fact that must be faced if citizens are to understand the stakes of modern politics."[5]

To this day, many people born after World War II are introduced to the history of the Holocaust by reading *Night*. And in some schools *Night* has replaced *The Diary of Anne Frank* as required reading. That would not have happened thirty or even twenty years ago. That time was too close to the actual event and people were still recovering from the shock.

The Diary of Anne Frank, written by a young girl who died in the Holocaust, is a sad but somewhat uplifting book. Anne wrote in her diary, "I still believe in the good of man."[6] But Wiesel's *Night* is dark and angry, and, as so many American publishers noted, it took a while for the public to be ready to deal with an unsparing account of such a sickening event in their lifetimes.

Ultimately, Wiesel was to become an American citizen and adopt the United States as his permanent home. His citizenship came about in an unplanned way. On a sweltering summer day in 1956, when he was living in New York City and covering the United Nations for *Yediot Aharonot*, Wiesel was struck by a taxi while he was crossing Times Square.

At first, there was a strong chance Wiesel would not survive. He suffered severe injuries, including numerous broken bones, and spent several weeks in the hospital. Following his release, he was confined to a wheelchair for nearly a year before he finally recovered from his injuries.

During the period when he was wheelchair-bound, Wiesel realized that his French visa was about to expire. He knew that a trip to France was necessary in order to have his visa extended, but in his physical condition there was no way he could make such a trip. Visits to the French consulate in New York and the U.S. immigration authorities were of no help.

Finally, at the suggestion of a U.S. immigration official, Wiesel solved his dilemma by becoming an American citizen, something he did with mixed emotions. In some ways he felt that since Israel was the official Jewish homeland, he belonged there, and he suspected that some Israeli citizens would resent his decision.

But he also knew that Jews living in Israel were

already familiar with the Holocaust, and that he would be able to do more good in a place where Jews were in the minority, as they are in the United States. He realized that it was more important that the word be spread to the rest of the world.

Soon afterward, Wiesel took a job as a writer of feature stories for a newspaper called the *Jewish Daily Forward,* published in New York. The paper had been founded in 1897 to serve the large number of eastern European Jews who had immigrated to the United States and it was written entirely in Yiddish, the native language for most of them. It was also, of course, Wiesel's native language. The *Forward* served for decades as a lifeline for newly settled Jews in the United States and continued to be published well into the 1980s.

Soon after the success of *Night* Wiesel's writing career began in earnest. He would never again write another fully autobiographical book like it. Instead, he wrote short novels.

Most writers of fiction write about what they know. Much of the time they use their own life experiences as a basis for their works, whether they be books, movie scripts, or stage plays. Wiesel, therefore, created main characters that had backgrounds similar to his own, then devised fictional plots, ideas, and supporting characters.

Wiesel actually began writing his second book before *Night* was published in France, but neither it nor his third book would be released in the United States until

1961 and 1962, after *Night* had already struck a chord with the people of western Europe and America. Both books were written in French and later translated into English.

The first was called *L'Aube*, published in English as *Dawn*. The hero, like the author, is a young Holocaust survivor. Unlike the author, however, the main character, named Elisha, ventures to Palestine to fight for the Jewish homeland that will become Israel. Elisha is ordered to kill an officer of the British occupation forces in reprisal for the death sentence ordered on a Jewish freedom fighter.

He feels no hostility toward his intended victim, yet he is told by superiors that the killing is an act of patriotism, that it is for the good of his people. Elisha wrestles with the concept of killing for his country; he has visions of his parents and teachers reprimanding him for the act. Against his own feelings, he goes through with the murder.

Shortly after writing *Dawn*, Wiesel wrote *Le Jour*, translated in English as *The Accident*. Here, he takes the premise of his own accident and expands upon it. The hero, Eliezer, is again a young Holocaust survivor who is hit by a car in New York. While recuperating in the hospital, he reflects on the mishap and begins to think that it was really a subconscious death wish.

Eliezer has lost faith in God and feels tremendous guilt for surviving the Holocaust while so many of his loved ones died. He ultimately wishes to die to join them. After failed attempts by his girlfriend and a surgeon to convince him otherwise, an artist friend belabors Eliezer for giving in to death.

Slowly but progressively, Eliezer begins to appreciate human kindness and love. Despite the fact that a merciful God is no longer a reality to him, he feels that the love of his friend and girlfriend are reasons enough to live.

Some might think that the writer actually had the same thoughts that his character, Eliezer, contemplated—that Wiesel felt his accident might have been a concealed death wish. But Wiesel denies it, saying the story was entirely a product of his creative imagination.

"It was really only an accident," he says. "I was crossing the street and the taxi went too fast and hit me. I used it as a pretext and wrote a novel about it and in my novel the main character felt it was a suicide attempt. But it was fiction."[7]

One pattern noticed by readers is that Wiesel commonly incorporates the letters *el* into his main characters' names. In Hebrew, *el* is a name for God.

7

Journeys to the Past

The paradoxes, or contradictions, in human nature have been a source of constant fascination to Wiesel and they have been a theme in several of his books. In 1960, when Wiesel was still working for *Yediot Aharonot*, he went to Jerusalem to cover the trial of a man named Adolf Eichmann, a former Nazi leader who had escaped to South America, only to be captured by the Israelis more than a decade later. Eichmann was brought to Israel to stand trial.

Eichmann had been accused of committing some of the most despicable crimes during the Holocaust, or, as stated by the prosecution in the trial, "crimes against humanity."[1] For his own protection, Eichmann was kept in a bulletproof glass box during the trial. So much anger was directed toward Eichmann that it was feared that someone would try to kill him before the trial ended.

To Wiesel's surprise, and to the amazement of many of the world's citizens watching coverage of the trial on television, this cold killer seemed so ordinary, almost meek and modest, wearing glasses and a plain suit inside his glass box.[2]

Eichmann was found guilty of his crimes and was put to death. Wiesel and the rest of the world discovered that evil comes in all forms, and that a mild-mannered presence can mask a villainous mind.

In the years following the trial Elie made several trips to Europe, to explore places important in either his past or that of the Jews in general. In some cases it was both. In 1962, he ventured to Germany for a short stay. It was his first time in Germany since the war and Elie went for two different reasons: to see the effect the legacy of the Holocaust had on the German people and to examine his own feelings.[3]

For seventeen years he had hated Germany and its people, but after this trip he found he had no more hatred. In its place he felt emptiness and sadness. The German people seemed to want to sweep the Holocaust and the awful memories of World War II under the rug. Hardly anyone there spoke of the subject. They felt no shame for what had happened, no self-disgust, no embarrassment.

Two years later, in the fall of 1964, Wiesel travelled

back to Sighet, to explore the streets and memories of his youngest days. Two decades had passed since the adolescent Elie Wiesel had been taken from his home, forced to board a train along with all the other Jews in the village.

In a touch of irony that is most appropriate, he arrived in Sighet at night. The village of his birth was once again part of Rumania, not Hungary, but was now one of several eastern European countries under Communist rule. The taxi dropped Wiesel off in the town square. He took a deep breath and drank in the sights, then walked through the streets until he found his childhood home.

Wiesel stood by the garden of the home where he grew up, where he studied and played chess, and where he enjoyed warm conversations with his grandfather, Dodye Feig. As he was remembering the tender days of his childhood, a sudden noise jolted him. It was a dog howling, and the abrupt sound in the middle of this autumn night made Wiesel flee from the site.

He passed a restless night outdoors in the town square and spent the next morning wandering around the town. He seemed invisible to the residents of Sighet, who had no idea who he was or what he was doing there. Wiesel's last stop before he left Sighet was a Jewish cemetery, where he recited a prayer for the deceased.[4]

Wiesel discussed his thoughts about his trip to Sighet in a book he wrote in 1970 called *One Generation After.*

It is a collection of essays and dialogues Wiesel has with himself, and the writing is more mystical and illusionary than that of *Night*.

In an essay called "Journey's Beginning," Wiesel wrote:

> Neighbors, acquaintances, friends: at times their presence becomes so real that I want to stop one of them, anyone, and entrust him with a message: Go and tell all those people, your companions and mine, tell them they're taking the wrong road, they're turning away from their future; tell them that danger lies in wait, that mankind is at their heels, hungry for their blood and their death.
>
> But I keep quiet. I am afraid lest that person reply:
>
> I don't believe you, I don't know you. Lest he shrug his shoulders and continue on the road straight to his tomb up there, his tomb veiled in incandescent clouds. I want to shout, to scream, only I am afraid of waking him. It is dangerous to wake the dead, especially if their memory is better than yours; it is dangerous to be seen by them, especially if they have robbed you of your town and childhood, the beginning you are remembering for the last time.[5]

Later on in *One Generation After*, Wiesel uses a bar mitzvah gift, a beautiful gold watch, as a metaphor, or symbol, of his lost childhood in an essay called "The Watch." The watch was meant to be a constant reminder that Elie, at thirteen years old, was now responsible for upholding the laws of the Torah.

But when the Nazis came with orders to force the Jews to leave Sighet, the Wiesel family buried all their valuables, including the watch, on the grounds of their home. His mother buried her silver candelabra, his father buried the family's valuable papers, and his little sister, Tzipora, buried her toys and school notebooks.

A total of twenty years later, when Wiesel returned to Sighet, he found himself in the garden of his boyhood home and he became curious to know if his watch was still where he buried it. So he dug with his fingers, and dug some more, breaking through frozen soil, digging faster and deeper and more fiercely, until he found the metal box he had placed his watch in such a long time ago.

He thought twice about opening the box, then gave in to his curiosity; but he found his once-treasured watch was rusted and filthy and covered with worms. At first, he was disgusted, but then he saw the watch as a survivor of the Holocaust, like himself. He wanted to take it home with him and have it repaired and regilded by "the best jeweler in the world."[6]

As he was leaving, Wiesel turned around, walked back to the garden, knelt down, put the watch back in the metal box, and buried it in the exact same spot. He said that some day another child would, by accident, dig up the watch. That child, Wiesel wrote, "would thus learn that his parents were usurpers, and that among the inhabitants of his town, there had been Jews and Jewish children, children robbed of their future."[7]

A year later, in 1965, Wiesel was on another faraway trip, this time to the Soviet Union. He had heard terrible stories about Jews in the USSR being persecuted under the Communist government and he planned a trip to see for himself. He intentionally scheduled his trip to coincide with the Jewish High Holidays, and the holiday of Sukkot, the Jewish harvest celebration which follows shortly afterward.

This way he could see for himself whether or not Jews were permitted to worship as they pleased. It was nearly impossible at that time for anyone to be permitted to emigrate from the USSR.

Wiesel planned to seek out and speak with average Jewish citizens, not with Jews who held important positions. But the Russian Jews found him before he discovered them. Because of Wiesel's clothing, Russians could tell he was a foreigner and only a few hours after his arrival he was approached outside a Moscow synagogue by a man who asked if he spoke Yiddish. The man hid his face, but exclaimed to Wiesel in Yiddish, "Do you know what is happening to us?"[8]

After Wiesel asked him to go into detail, the stranger responded, "There is no time. We are nearing the end. Impossible to give you details. You must understand. If I am being watched I will pay for this conversation. Do not forget."[9]

The man was scared, so scared that he wouldn't even shake Wiesel's hand.[10] He slipped away, in the middle of a sentence, and lost himself in the masses of people crowding the entrance of the synagogue.

Wiesel was to have similar encounters throughout his trip. In the middle of a religious service, a man sitting near the visitor told him in Hebrew that anti-Semitism was rampant and that Jews weren't even allowed to teach Jewish law to their children. The worshiper was careful to sneak his own forbidden words into the middle of a prayer, so that government authorities monitoring the service wouldn't catch on.

On other occasions, a fearful Jew would hurriedly push a note in Wiesel's pocket, or just knowingly wink an eye at him. Wiesel knew by now what the Russian Jews wanted, but were forbidden to say. He was soon to learn that Soviet Jews were fearful not only of the government, but also of one another, believing that some of their fellow worshipers were really Jewish informers working for the Soviet secret police.

Any number of times—in Moscow, in Leningrad, and particularly in Kiev—I was cautioned by a wink or a low whisper, "Watch out for that one; he works for them." Their suspicion can reach the pitch of terror. No one trusts anyone.[11]

Wiesel discussed the results of his trip in *The Jews of Silence*, which was published in 1966. The book spearheaded interest in Soviet Jewry among both Jews and Gentiles; one of the latter was Senator Henry Jackson of Washington State, who became a leading spokesman for the right of Soviet Jews to emigrate.

Depending on the fickle mood of the Soviet Communist leadership, over the period from the early 1970s until the fall of communism Jews were allowed in varying numbers to leave the USSR. Their common choices were the United States or Israel, two countries where they could live openly as Jews without fear of reprisal.

When not on the road, Wiesel devoted most of his time to his passion: writing. Based roughly upon the experiences of the Moscow rabbi whose synagogue he attended for Kol Nidre (eve of Yom Kippur) services, Wiesel wrote *Zalmen, or the Madness of God*, his first stage play. Unlike a tormented Russian rabbi who in real life remained silent, the rabbi in this work of fiction lashes out at the system and its inherent prejudices against Jews, speaking his mind, announcing to the public his fears and his concerns.

In 1968, Wiesel wrote a collection of short stories and essays called *Legends of Our Time*, in which he pays tribute to those people who meant most to him, including his father and his teachers. In 1969, one person who would indeed fall into that category was a woman named Marion Erster Rose. Wiesel married her just before Passover of that, his thirty-ninth year.

Marion, like Elie, was a concentration camp survivor. In contrast to his seriousness, she was bubbly and lively. She had been married before and had a daughter named Jennifer from her earlier marriage. It was appropriate that Wiesel was married in spring, the traditional time of rebirth and renewal, because the marriage itself was a kind of renewal for his long, lonely life.

It was to Marion that Wiesel dedicated his next book, *A Beggar in Jerusalem,* and it was his most celebrated work since *Night.* It was first released in Europe, where it won a prestigious honor called the Prix Médicis and sold over 10,000 copies, and after this tremendous reception, *A Beggar in Jerusalem* was published in the United States in 1970.

The novel parallels the story of the Jewish people in the 20th century with that of an Israeli soldier and Holocaust survivor named David and his friend, Katriel. David survives the Six-Day War between the Arabs and Israelis in 1967, although his best friend, Katriel, is lost, just as the Jewish people and the nation of Israel have survived even though many individuals have not.

As with Wiesel's other books, a theme of *A Beggar in Jerusalem* is the awfulness of war. (The reference in the following excerpt to "the Wall" is to the Western Wall, the only surviving remnant of Solomon's temple in Jerusalem. Religious Jews believe that written notes slipped between the cracks in the Wall are messages sent directly to God. They believe that the presence of God hovers over the massive wall. If you ever visit Jerusalem you will see scads of paper of all shapes and sizes tucked carefully into the stone wall's many cracks):

> Somewhere a storyteller is bent over a photograph taken by a German, an officer fond of collecting souvenirs. It shows a father and son, in the middle of a human herd, moving toward a ditch where, a moment later, they will be shot. The father, his left hand on the boy's shoulder, speaks to him gently while his right hand points to the sky. He is explaining the battle between love and hatred: "You see, my child, we are right now losing that battle." And since the boy does not answer, his father continues: "Know, my son, if gratuitous suffering exists, it is ordained by divine will. Whoever kills, becomes God. Whoever kills, kills God. Each murder is a suicide, with the Eternal eternally the victim."
>
> And the survivor in all this? He will end up writing his request, which he will slip between the cracks of the Wall. Addressed to the dead, it will ask them to take pity on a world which has betrayed and rejected them. Being powerful and vindictive, they can do whatever they please. Punish. Or even forgive.[12]

The Professor and the Presidents

Professor Elie Wiesel has been teaching classes in literature and philosophy at Boston University since 1976. He holds the title of Andrew W. Mellon Professor in the Humanities at that urban campus. But his career in the academic world began four years earlier, in 1972, when he was named Distinguished Professor of Judaic Studies at City University of New York (CUNY) in Manhattan.

At that time Wiesel taught the Holocaust. His class was incredibly popular and on many occasions his students were children of survivors. One might think such young people would learn all they need to know from their parents. But while they might learn some facts and true-life experiences, these young men and women, raised in a country where government oppression does not exist and people are free to worship as they please, might not understand their parents' innermost feelings, their anxiousness, apprehensions, and fears.

Classes were intense. Emotions often overtook rational and objective discussion, since the subject is both so horrible and still fairly recent. To Wiesel, it transcends other tragedies of human existence.

The Holocaust is singular, in that it epitomizes in quality and quantity the degree of hatred that can be perpetrated against a different people simply because they *are* different. The victims were innocent people, going about their daily lives, who were simply herded up and murdered in an attempt to destroy every one of them with no regard for the individual.

In an interview with *Reform Judaism* magazine, Wiesel said, "The Holocaust is a sacred subject. One should take off one's shoes when entering its domain. One should tremble each time one pronounces the word."[1]

When Wiesel accepted the Boston University position in 1976 he ceased teaching the Holocaust at CUNY. He still lives in New York, however, and commutes to Boston by air. About the time he began teaching at CUNY, Wiesel started a regular lecture series at New York City's 92nd Street YM-YWHA (Young Men's-Young Women's Hebrew Association). The series continues today.

Elie Wiesel teaching class at Boston University. He began his tenure
at the university in 1976.

Throughout the 1970s Wiesel continued to write. His book, *Souls on Fire*, was filled with essays about Hasidism, based in part about his lectures at the Y. *The Oath*, a semiautobiographical novel about an entire village which takes a vow of silence following a pogrom (an organized killing spree of Jews), was published in 1973. In *The Oath*, the pogrom's sole survivor breaks his vow of silence to save another life; Wiesel appears to be confirming the notion that people must speak up when the well-being of others is at stake.

Survival of the Jews has always been a foremost priority in Wiesel's mind, but he never knew if he wanted children of his own. He wasn't sure if he could justify bringing a child in the world that was so cruel to him.[2] On June 6, 1972, however, a son was born to Elie and Marion Wiesel. The boy was named Shlomo Elisha, Shlomo being Wiesel's father's name, and Elisha after the Hebrew prophet of the Bible, whose name means "God is salvation."

Wiesel said in *The New York Times* in 1973 that fifteen years earlier he hadn't been emotionally ready to have a child or even to get married. Even after Shlomo Elisha's arrival into the world, Wiesel told the *Times*:

> When he was born I felt very sorry for him. I felt sorry for him coming into this ugly, difficult, horrible world. Now I still feel sympathy, but naturally the urge is much stronger than before to

try to do what we can to make it a little better. Because he is here, we try.

We believe in names so much. I was the only son. I cannot break the chain. It is impossible that 3,500 years should end with me, so I took these 3,500 years and put them on the shoulders of this little child. It took me some time to realize the outrageous courage that it takes to have a child today.[3]

A haunting image that has never left Wiesel's memory is that of bystanders watching Jews in Europe being forced to board cattle cars that were to transport them on a ride to doom. Those who do not speak up when injustice takes place, those who are indifferent, says Wiesel, are guilty as collaborators. He calls indifference a sin.[4]

By the mid-1970s, many non-Jewish people around the globe began to claim that they had heard enough about the Holocaust. Perhaps some may think all has been said that can be said about the subject. Perhaps, because they themselves aren't Jewish, many people can't relate to the deep feelings Jews across the world have about the topic. Maybe some people just find it too depressing and want to think about happier things.

But some are simply bigots. Called revisionists, since they are revising the truth, these people claim the Holocaust never happened. The revisionists say that the story of the Holocaust is all part of some massive conspiracy made up by Jews to gain the world's sympathy and monetary compensation. They say people like Elie Wiesel are liars.

So, in 1978, Wiesel accepted the invitation of President Jimmy Carter to head the President's Commission on the Holocaust, which would soon become known as the Holocaust Memorial Council. He would hold the post until 1986.

Wiesel was sworn into his new office by Speaker of the House Thomas P. (Tip) O'Neill on February 15, 1979, on an 18th-century Jewish Bible that the Nazis had once looted from a German synagogue. At the time he said:

> The problems facing us may seem insurmountable. We are supposed to remember and move others to remember, but how does one remember individually and collectively an event that was intended to erase memory?
>
> All the documents, all the testimony, all the eyewitness accounts, all the history books notwithstanding, we know that we have not yet begun to tell the tale.
>
> How does one reconcile the purely Jewish aspects of the tragedy with its inevitable universal connotations?[5]

One of the commission's initial ideas was the planning of a museum and library devoted to the Holocaust in Washington, D.C., which opened in April, 1993. Another concept the commission developed was that of an annual Day of Remembrance, to help instill

Elie Wiesel meets with President Jimmy Carter. In 1978, Carter asked Wiesel to head the President's Commission on the Holocaust.

the memory of the Holocaust in the minds of people who feel it is worth forgetting, and to counter those who declare that it never happened.

The first Day of Remembrance took place on April 24, 1979. In the United States Capitol Wiesel spoke before hundreds of onlookers, who included President Carter and both houses of Congress. Speaking in the third person, he told how almost thirty-five years ago to the day his family was taken from their home. He said he asked his father if it was all part of a nightmare. These things don't happen in this day and age.

Wiesel recalled that he said to his father, "If this were true, the world would not be silent."

His father replied, "Perhaps the world does not know."

Wiesel continued, in his speech to the gathered audience, "The world knew and kept silent."

He then thanked President Carter for remembering. "Memory may perhaps be our only answer, our only hope to save the world from ultimate punishment, a nuclear holocaust."[6]

Later that summer, Elie and the other members of the commission and their families, including many who were not Jewish, flew to Europe to remember at the actual scenes of the terror, then on to the Soviet Union and Israel. Stops included the former concentration and death camp sites at Treblinka, Auschwitz, and Birkenau.

President Jimmy Carter and Elie Wiesel (front row, from left) took part in the first Day of Remembrance on April 24, 1979.

It was Wiesel's first trip back to the Soviet Union since *The Jews of Silence* was published.

In Ukraine, the commission visited Babi Yar, a ravine outside Kiev, where in 1941 the Nazis slaughtered more than 100,000 people, of whom about 35,000 were Jews. The visitors noticed that while the Soviet government had placed a monument to the dead at the site, this did not mention the fact that many of the victims were murdered simply because they were Jewish. The writing on the monument memorialized the Soviet citizens who were killed, but did not commemorate the Jews at all.

In Israel, the commission paused at Yad Vashem, the nation's national shrine and research center remembering the Holocaust and its victims. The monument, opened in 1957, is centered around a solemn, simple structure called the Tent of Remembrance, highlighted by an eternal flame, illuminated in memory of the Holocaust victims.

Embedded in the floor are the names of death camps. Leading to the memorial is a pathway called the Avenue of the Righteous, where non-Jews who risked their lives to help Jews escape the Nazis are memorialized by living trees. Many of these righteous Gentiles did not survive.

Not every stop on the trip was to remember the evil. In Denmark, the commission paid tribute to a man named Raoul Wallenburg, a Swedish statesman who is

Inside the Tent of Remembrance at Yad Vashem. An eternal flame
highlights the structure, in memory of the Holocaust victims.

immortalized on the Avenue of the Righteous. He is credited as saving approximately 30,000 innocent Jews in Nazi-held Hungary. Wallenberg disappeared after being arrested by the Soviet army when they captured Hungary. His whereabouts have never been confirmed. (The Soviet government maintains that he died in one of their prisons in 1947.) A proclamation honoring Wallenberg was presented by the commission to his sister.

The next year Wiesel showed the world that his sympathies extended to oppressed people who aren't Jewish when he traveled to Southeast Asia with an international group of humanitarians. The purpose was to deliver food, medicine, and other needed supplies to Cambodian refugees, victims of war and famine that followed the expulsion of their murderous leader, Pol Pot. Elie Wiesel's group tried to cross the border from Thailand into Cambodia, but was stopped by border guards.

They sat down in silent protest, then Wiesel stood and, along with American Rabbi Marc Tanenbaum and other Jews, chanted the Jewish prayer called Kaddish, the prayer for the dead. It had been thirty-five years ago to the day, according to the Jewish calendar, that Shlomo Wiesel, his father, died in Buchenwald. But, in a way, he was also saying the prayer for those dead and dying across the border in Cambodia.

Raoul Wallenberg sitting at his desk in Budapest, Hungary. He is credited with saving approximately 30,000 innocent Jews in Nazi-held Hungary.

Wiesel was quoted in the February 7, 1980 *New York Times* as saying:

> I came here because nobody came when I was there. One thing that is worse for the victim than hunger, fear, torture, even humiliation, is the feeling of abandonment, the feeling that nobody cares, the feeling that you don't count. I have absolutely no right not to be here. Perhaps we cannot change the world, but I do not want the world to change me.[7]

A day later, the Red Cross distributed the supplies to the refugees.

To counter the revisionists, a World Gathering of Jewish Holocaust Survivors was held in Jerusalem in June, 1981. Nearly 7,000 survivors and their families attended and Elie served as honorary chairman of the event.

Wiesel has received his share of awards and commendations, like the Eleanor Roosevelt Award and the Martin Luther King Medallion. But an awards ceremony at the White House in 1985 made him a household name, as well as a figure of controversy, to many who had previously been unfamiliar with his work.

That year, Wiesel traveled to Washington, D.C., to accept the Congressional Medal of Achievement personally from President Ronald Reagan. But this was not to be an ordinary, uneventful awards ceremony. Wiesel had learned that President Reagan would soon be taking a trip to West Germany, where he would be

In 1985, Elie Wiesel met with President Ronald Reagan to accept
the Congressional Medal of Achievement.

laying a memorial wreath at Bitburg Military Cemetery. Those buried at Bitburg included members of the notorious Nazi SS. Wiesel was appalled that the president of the United States would honor the ground where vicious murderers were buried.

While at the podium, Wiesel took advantage of his unique audience with the president to plead with him to change his plans and not stop at Bitburg. "That place, Mr. President, is not your place. Your place is with the victims of the SS," he implored, then continued:

> The issue here is not politics, but good and evil. And we must never confuse them. For I have seen the SS at work and I have seen their victims. They were my friends. They were my parents. Mr. President, there was a degree of suffering in the concentration camps that defies imagination.[8]

Some Americans were upset that the recipient of a medal would lecture the president. Others felt that Wiesel's plea was gracious and dignified. Most American Jews were proud of what Wiesel did, some deeming it one of the shining moments of Jewish American history.

Years later, Wiesel was asked if he felt any discomfort speaking to the president that day:

> No, he answered, because I had had a relationship with him before. Also, it is rare that you are so sure of the cause you are defending, and I was sure.
>
> Furthermore, I went out of my way to be fair. I even sent him my speech beforehand. I didn't have to. I have much respect for the position of President

of the United States, in addition to a very good relationship, so I felt I had no problem."[9]

President Reagan made the trip and on May 5, 1986, he and West German Chancellor Helmut Kohl went ahead with their planned visit to Bitburg Military Cemetery.

Wiesel recalled, "[Reagan] said he couldn't go back on his promise, that Kohl insisted. It really was Kohl's fault, except the President of the United States should be strong enough to stand up to Kohl."[10]

As a result of the Bitburg affair, Kohl organized an informal group of Germans and American Jews to discuss their feelings forty years after the Holocaust ended. Wiesel was invited to take part, and did so. Afterward, he urged reconciliation between Jews and the new generation of young Germans, who acknowledged the wrongs of their country's past.

But another, even greater honor, was soon to be Wiesel's. About five o'clock in the morning on October 14, 1986, the phone range in his New York apartment. The call was from a Norwegian named Jakob Sverdrup, the director of the Nobel Institute, who informed Wiesel that he had been selected as the winner of the Nobel Peace Prize. The date also happened to be close to Yom Kippur.

Later that day, Wiesel said of the news, "I was of course very stunned and grateful, and melancholy. I fell back into the mood of Yom Kuppur—serious reflections

While accepting the Congressional Medal of Achievement award, Elie Wiesel took the opportunity to voice his views about President Reagan's planned trip to Bitburg.

about my parents and my grandparents. It took me a half hour to get out of it."[11]

Within a week after winning the Nobel Prize, Wiesel traveled to Moscow to speak about the millions of non-Jewish civilians and prisoners of war who were also killed by the Nazis. Two months later, he took another long trip, this time to Oslo, Norway, to receive his prized honor from the Nobel Committee. During his acceptance speech, Wiesel brought his fourteen-year-old son to the podium, to demonstrate the fact that despite years of oppression Jews continue to survive.

9

To Remember

Today, Wiesel is as active and busy as ever. He wakes early in his New York apartment, a habit held over from his days as a young child in Sighet. He writes for four hours each day, except on the Sabbath and Jewish holidays, and he starts as early as 5:30 in the morning.

Wiesel still teaches at Boston University, commuting from his home twice a week. Students sign up a year or more in advance to take Wiesel's courses. Most of those lucky enough to get a spot are upperclassmen or graduate students enrolled at the university.

However, it's not unusual to find a divinity student from nearby Harvard University, an area priest, a college student from Germany, or a Jesuit priest from France who has moved to Boston temporarily among the group taking his class. They come not only to learn about the topic at hand, but to drink in Wiesel's sentiments, hoping some of his humanitarian views will rub off.

When asked what message he has for young people, Wiesel answers immediately:

> To be sensitive. Education means to sensitize. Memory means to sensitize. Involvement means to be sensitive already. To be sensitive to other people's joy, other people's fear, other people's suffering, other people's lives. We are responsible for ourselves and for others.[1]

One of his long-time teaching assistants, Janet McCord, says, "There are many Protestant ministers out there who are so taken with his work that they use stories from his works as sermon illustrations."[2]

Lyle Linder, a Methodist minister from Nebraska, says that Wiesel's presence at Boston University was a key reason he chose to travel such a long distance to Boston to study for his doctorate. Linder explains:

> Elie Wiesel has a great compassion for all suffering people who are oppressed and victimized. I have read his books over the years and have always been struck by his moral commitment, his ethics, and his spirituality.
>
> He is so interested in his students, he loves to dialogue with his students. His graciousness pours out of him. The other day he flew back from Paris just to make his class.[3]

Wiesel teaches several subjects relating to literature,

Elie Wiesel teaches several subjects relating to literature. Here, he engages students in conversation.

although there is one author he will never discuss: himself.

He explains, "I don't teach the Holocaust. I'm not here to promote myself."[4]

Though he is a small, slight man with a soft voice and thick European accent, Wiesel commands a classroom. He leans against the back of a chair as he engages his students in conversation, asking questions and offering comments and responding to students' reactions.

The subjects are usually serious ones. In one class devoted to the writings of Franz Kafka, an Austrian author who wrote in the early part of this century, Wiesel discusses the antiwar message of one of Kafka's novels, *The Trial.* In a severe tone, he states, "War is the most terrifying, bloodiest, cruelest, most dangerous game the world has invented for its children."[5]

This survivor makes such a statement from personal experience, something few others in his position can do.

Yet neither the professor nor his class are all pensiveness and somberness, although that is the image that Wiesel publicly projects. Joe Kanofsky, another of Wiesel's teaching assistants, says:

> When people hear that I work with Professor Wiesel, they say, 'We see him on television speaking and he seems so serious.'
> But you don't know him until you see his eyes light up and you've seen him crack a smile. He's

got a wonderful sense of humor and loves a good joke, never at anyone's expense, but always about something touching on human nature. People who haven't had his classes don't see him in that mood."[6]

For example, in the Kafka class, Wiesel discusses the significance of two men shaking hands in a scene from a book. He departs from his heavy tone for a moment, looks up and says, incidentally, that he recently read that for people who have colds, shaking hands is more unsanitary than kissing.

"Not that I'm suggesting anything," he smiles.[7]

His teaching assistants stress that despite his fame and worldwide respect, Professor Wiesel's students do not seem to be intimidated by having him as a teacher. In fact, he seems to go out of his way not to make his students fearful.

"He is a very gentlemanly, very welcoming, warm person," comments Joe Kanofsky. "It might be intimidating learning with someone else of that stature, but not with Professor Wiesel."[8]

Janet McCord responds, "Yes, students [initially] get nervous but Professor Wiesel puts them at ease. Even if they are wrong about something he'll tell them that they are wrong, but he does it in such a nice way that he doesn't embarrass them. I've never seen him embarrass anyone."[9]

His personal assistant, Martha Hauptman, has been

with him since the late 1970s. She has witnessed students come and go, often hearing such comments as, "This was the best class in my entire four years at Boston University," or "Studying with Professor Wiesel changed my life."

"Sometimes," Hauptman says, "students headed in a particular direction will completely shift the course they are on to pursue something different, perhaps a more humane endeavor."[10]

Since winning the Nobel Prize, Wiesel's presence is more in demand than ever. He still offers regular lectures at the 92nd Street YM-YWHA in Manhattan, and he gives three lectures a year at Boston University. Those who hear him speak are part of a very fortunate group since there are constant requests for him to share his knowledge with audiences in the United States and other countries.

Elie Wiesel, the man himself, has hardly changed since he won the Nobel Prize. Says Martha Hauptman:

> He's the same *mensch* [Yiddish word for a person of character and moral strength] that he was from the very beginning, just maybe more tired. The demands upon him have increased tremendously, perhaps the demands he puts upon himself as well.
>
> One noticeable change I see is the way others regard him. People tend to pay more attention to individuals who have won the Nobel Peace Prize. I think that his words are taken more seriously and that people listen with more interest and respect.

Surely, his renown throughout the world has increased since then, as has the volume of mail received from places far and wide.[11]

There are other Holocaust survivors who have made a career of fighting hatred. Many do not have Wiesel's fame, but they praise his example. Elane Norych Geller works out of the Simon Wiesenthal Center, a human rights agency in Los Angeles. She spent almost five years as a child, from age four and a half to nine, in concentration camps during World War II. Today, she lectures to schoolchildren and others about her experiences, encouraging brotherhood among all people.

Geller says that Wiesel has been a great influence on her:

He has given me a lot of inspiration, without question. As a survivor I have always been grateful for his eloquence.

She adds,

The journey of being a survivor, a child survivor, is a very lonely one. And for such a very long time many survivors, I being one, were reluctant to speak out. I was in the camps at such a young age that I was able to defer dealing with it, and chose to do it in a certain way. And if there was any subconscious guilt that I wasn't speaking up as I matured, there was always the knowledge that someone like Wiesel was speaking for me, and for all of us.[12]

Of course, like every prominent person, Wiesel has his share of detractors. Some Jewish critics like writers

Alfred Kazin and Irving Howe have claimed that he has capitalized on his unfortunate status as a Holocaust victim and is more interested in publicity for himself than the causes he champions.

Kazin once ridiculed Wiesel by calling him a "professional survivor," and Howe was quoted in *The New Republic*, saying that "the grief he [Wiesel] declares, surely sincere, is alloyed by streaks of publicity,"[13] Martin Peretz, the magazine's editor has been particularly critical of Wiesel for similar reasons. Peretz once ran an article in his magazine ridiculing a Boston University campaign supporting Wiesel's Nobel Peace Prize.

In response, a staff member of *The New Republic* admitted to the *Boston Globe* that many of the magazine's readers found Peretz's criticisms offensive. Acknowledging all the positive work Wiesel has done, the staff member apologized by saying, "There are a lot worse people to go after than Elie Wiesel."[14]

There has been a reaction by some that Wiesel has hesitated to speak up when those who aren't Jewish are being oppressed. This argument is simply not true.

For instance, Wiesel has spoken out against abuses of Arab protesters by Israeli soldiers. In an editorial that ran in *The New York Times* on June 23, 1988, he wrote, "I understand the anger of young Palestinians. Frustrated, diminished, disappointed, they feel cheated and unwanted by society, betrayed by the whole world, including the Arab world. They are treated as non-persons."[15]

Other examples of his work for non-Jews include the attention he has brought to human rights violations in other countries and, of course, his 1980 trip to bring relief supplies to Cambodia.

And he has taken the time to praise Christians like the brave Swedish diplomat, Raoul Wallenberg, who risked their lives to save Jews from the Nazis. Wiesel wrote an article in the April 6, 1985, issue of *TV Guide* to elaborate on a made-for-television movie about the life of Wallenberg. In it he discussed the heroism of Wallenberg and other righteous Gentiles. One was a Bulgarian named Dimon Kazasov who helped halt German plans to send Bulgarian Jews to death camps. Another was King Christian X of Denmark, who it is said wore a yellow star in solidarity with the Jews of his country. Christian X joined with the Danish people in an effort to save threatened Jews by evacuating them to Sweden. A third righteous Gentile was an Italian monk named Father Rufino Niccacci who hid 300 Italian Jews from the Nazis. Wiesel's main criticism is that there aren't enough of these inspiring stories to tell.

Wiesel stresses involvement when he gives his message to others. In interview after interview, he says that those who do not take a part in reacting to and stopping oppression are as guilty as the actual oppressors.

And there are those hatemongers, the revisionist

bigots who insist that the Holocaust never happened. The Ku Klux Klan in the United States, and in both Europe and America, neo-Nazis—people who support Hitler's ideas—are among those who spread these rumors. Wiesel says he first heard of this movement in the early 1970s and he hears from these people to this day. In fact, he adds, supporters of this distasteful cause protested outside the hall in Oslo when he was accepting his Nobel Peace Prize.

As for how to deal with such bigots, teaching assistant Joe Kanofsky brings up an important point. "It is a very difficult situation to enter into because once you debate these people you lend their argument credence by saying, 'All right, we'll debate this in a civilized forum.' And it's quite an uncivilized argument they're making."[16]

Wiesel admits that he still has nightmares about his year in the concentration camps, nearly fifty years after it occurred, but he has fewer as time passes.[17] It's something he doesn't like to discuss.

"It's a very personal thing," he says.[18]

What if he had never spent his terrible year in the Holocaust? Wiesel says he would still be a writer and teacher, but his chosen subjects would be a bit different. "I would have taught Talmud and written commentaries on religious texts."[19]

Since being awarded the Nobel Peace Prize, he and Marion Wiesel began their Wiesel Foundation for

Humanity. The Wiesels have sponsored conferences on various topics across the world. A recent subject has been the analysis of hate, trying to examine why people hate, and discussing what can be done to control hate.

Elie has also founded the Elie Wiesel Prize in Ethics, an essay contest for university students, and Marion Wiesel has been involved in working with Ethiopian children in Israel. Because of oppression and famine, many Ethiopian Jews were rescued by the Israelis.

Like a river that keeps flowing, Elie Wiesel keeps writing. In 1992, his book *The Forgotten* was published, bringing the total of books he has written to well over thirty. In a way, *The Forgotten* closes a cycle that began with *Night*. While the emphasis of *Night* is on the vow never to forget, the main character in *The Forgotten,* an elderly Holocaust survivor named Elhanan, suffers from Alzheimer's disease, an illness that affects the memory. Elhanan trusts his son to keep his memories alive.

Wiesel told *Publisher's Weekly* in 1992 that he took some time to compare all his works:

> What do they have in common? he asked himself. Their commitment to memory. What is the opposite of memory? Alzheimer's disease. I began to research this topic and I discovered that this is the worst disease, that every intellectual is afraid of this disease, not just because it is incurable, which is true of other diseases, too. But here the identity is being abolished. And so I do not see it as a disease, I see it as a malediction."[20]

Elie Wiesel accepts the Congressional Medal of Freedom from President George Bush in 1992.

Typically, in his Nobel Prize acceptance speech, Wiesel repeatedly used the words, "I remember."[21] For those who are too young to remember, or might otherwise have forgotten, Elie Wiesel makes sure they don't forget. Through his writings and his teachings, he keeps the horrible memory of what happened to him and so many others alive, and warns that unless all people retain such memories, similar events can happen again.

In fact, in 1992 it appeared that history was repeating itself in the former country of Yugoslavia. The nation, located along the Adriatic Sea in eastern Europe, was formed as a union of several independent republics following World War I. However, after the fall of communism, some of the republics declared their independence. Many had been at odds with each other for centuries and without the cohesion of a unified republic, warfare broke out between the varied groups of people.

What troubled many observers from all over the world was the theory of "ethnic cleansing," espoused by the people of Serbia, one of the newly declared republics. This meant that the Serbs were trying forcibly to remove from their land any person who was not what they considered a true Serb. Serbia had also been accused of supporting a campaign of terror against Muslims in the neighboring republic of Bosnia. This included the indiscriminate raping of women and torture of children and other civilians.

To many people, this seemed much like the Nazi campaign against the Jews. Noticing this, Wiesel made a trip to Bosnia in November, 1992, and voiced his outrage at the situation.

In April 1993, at the dedication of the United States Holocaust Memorial Museum in Washington, D.C., Wiesel spoke in the strongest terms, denouncing the ethnic cleansing taking place in former Yugoslavia.

"We cannot tolerate the excruciating sights of this old new war," he exclaimed. Turning to President Bill Clinton, Wiesel urged, "Mr. President, this bloodshed must be stopped. It will not unless we stop it."[22]

Wiesel also discussed the importance of the museum, as well as his own personal connection to the Holocaust. He told the story of a Jewish woman in the Carpathian Mountains in 1943 who read an article in the local newspaper about a rebellion of Jews in Warsaw, Poland, an event that came to be known as the Warsaw Ghetto Uprising. Wiesel said, "She wondered aloud: 'Why are our Jews in Warsaw behaving like this? Why are they fighting? Couldn't they have waited quietly until the end of the war?' "

This woman, Wiesel noted, was unaware of what was happening to the Jews of Europe. She didn't know what the Jews in Warsaw were fighting against. Wiesel continued by naming concentration and death camps: "Treblinka, Ponar, Belzec, Chelmno, Birkenau; she had never heard of these places. One year later, together with

Elie Wiesel (right), with Harvey M. Meyerhoff, chairman of the Holocaust Memorial Council, and President Bill Clinton, attends the dedication of the United States Holocaust Memorial Museum in April, 1993.

her entire family, she was in a cattle car traveling to the black hole of history named Auschwitz.

"She was my mother," Wiesel said, concluding his speech.[23]

There is a common saying: "He who does not remember history is bound to repeat it." Elie Wiesel wants to be sure that that never happens again.

Chronology

1928—Eliezer Wiesel born to Shlomo and Sarah Wiesel in village of Sighet in Transylvania.

1944—With his family, taken prisoner by Nazis and placed in Auschwitz concentration camp.

1945—Elie's father dies but Elie is rescued by the Allies from Buchenwald concentration camp.

Taken with other child survivors to an orphanage in France.

Takes vow of silence not to write about his experiences for ten years.

1946—Leaves orphanage, moves to Paris on his own.

1948—Hired as Paris correspondent by Israeli newspaper, *Yediot Aharonot.*

1954—Meets French writer François Mauriac, who urges him to break vow of silence.

1956—Severely injured in auto accident in New York City.

Takes job writing for *Jewish Daily Forward.*

1958—First book, *Night,* published in France.

1960—*Night* published in English in the United States.

1961—Second book, *Dawn,* published in the United States.

1962— *The Accident* published in the United States.

1963—Naturalized full citizen of the United States.

1964—Returns to Sighet for first time since his capture by the Nazis.

1965—First trip to the Soviet Union.

1966—*The Jews of Silence*, based on Soviet Union trip, is published.

1969—Marries Marion Erster Rose, also a Holocaust survivor.

1970—*A Beggar in Jerusalem* is published in the United States.

1972—Son, Shlomo Elisha Wiesel, born.

1972-1976—Named Professor of Judaic Studies at City University of New York.

1976—Named Andrew W. Mellon Professor of the Humanities at Boston University.

1979—Sworn in as Chairman of President's Commission on the Holocaust.

1980—Visits former concentration camps with members of commission.

1980-1981—Humanitarian trip to Southeast Asia to help Cambodian refugees.

1985—Accepts Congressional Medal of Achievement. Urges President Reagan not to visit Bitburg.

1986—Awarded Nobel Peace Prize.

1987—Founds Elie and Marion Wiesel Foundation for Humanity.

1988—Elie Wiesel Awards for Jewish Arts and Culture established by B'nai Brith Hillel Foundations.

1990—Awarded the first Raoul Wallenberg Medal from the University of Michigan.

1992—Publishes *The Forgotten.*

1993—A principal speaker at dedication of United States Holocaust Memorial Museum, Washington, D.C.

Chapter Notes

Chapter 1

1. Elie Wiesel, *Against Silence*, ed. Irving Abrahamson (New York: Holocaust Library, 1985), vol. 1, p. 185.

2. "Wiesel's Speech at Nobel Ceremony," *New York Times*, December 11, 1986, p. A12.

3. Francis X. Clines, "Wiesel, Accepting the Nobel, Asks the Living to Remember," *New York Times*, December 11, 1986, p. 1.

Chapter 2

1. Personal interview with Elie Wiesel, November 2, 1992.

2. Ibid.

3. Ellen Norman Stern, *Elie Wiesel: Witness for Life* (New York: Ktav Publishing House, 1982), p. 14.

4. Elie Wiesel, *A Jew Today (Dodye Feig, A Portrait)* (New York: Vintage Books, 1978), pp. 75–82.

5. Ibid., p. 77.

6. Personal interview with Elie Wiesel, November 2, 1992.

7. Stern, p. 20.

8. Ibid., pp. 25–26.

9. Ibid., pp. 24–25.

Chapter 3

1. Martin Gilbert, *The Holocaust* (New York: Holt, Rinehart & Winston, 1985), p. 442.

Chapter 4

1. The information for this chapter comes from Elie Wiesel, *Night* (New York, Hill and Wang, 1960).

Excerpts from *Night* by Elie Wiesel, and excerpts from François Mauriac's introduction to *Night*. Copyright © 1960 by MacGibbon & Kee. Copyright renewed © 1988 by the Collins Publishing Group. Reprinted by permission of Hill and Wang, a division of Farrar, Straus & Giroux, Inc.

Chapter 5

1. Ellen Norman Stern, *Elie Wiesel: Witness for Life* (New York: Ktav Publishing House, 1982), pp. 97–98.

2. Ibid., p. 108.

3. Personal interview with Elie Wiesel, November 2, 1992.

4. Samuel J. Freedman, "Bearing Witness, The Life and Work of Elie Wiesel," *New York Times Magazine,* October 23, 1983, p. 66.

5. Personal interview with Elie Wiesel, November 2, 1992.

Chapter 6

1. Elie Wiesel, *Night,* intro. by François Mauriac (New York: Hill and Wang, 1960), pp. VII, VIII.

2. Elie Wiesel, *Against Silence,* ed. Irving Abrahamson (New York: Holocaust Library, 1985), vol. 3, pp. 68–69.

3. Samuel J. Freedman, "Bearing Witness, The Life and Work of Elie Wiesel," *New York Times Magazine,* October 23, 1983, p. 66.

4. Jonathan Dorfman, "The Paradox of Elie Wiesel," *Boston Globe,* March 13, 1991, p. 78.

5. Irving Abrahamson, "Elie Wiesel: Speaking Truth to Power," *Reform Judaism*, Fall 1985, p. 27.

6. Anne Frank, *Anne Frank: The Diary of a Young Girl* (New York: Simon & Schuster Pocket Books, 1958), p. VII.

7. Personal interview with Elie Wiesel, November 2, 1992.

Chapter 7

1. Moshe Perlman, *The Capture and Trial of Adolf Eichmann* (New York: Simon & Schuster, 1963), pp. 632–643.

2. Elie Wiesel, *One Generation After* (New York: Schocken Books, 1970), pp. 5–6.

3. Elie Wiesel, *Legends of Our Time* (New York: Schocken Books, 1968), pp. 131–132.

4. Elie Wiesel, *Against Silence*, ed. Irving Abrahamson (New York: Holocaust Library, 1985), vol. 3., pp. 68–69.

5. Wiesel, *One Generation After*, p. 13.

6. Ibid., pp. 60–65.

7. Ibid., p. 64.

8. Elie Wiesel, *The Jews of Silence* (New York: Schocken Books, 1966), p. 8.

9. Ibid.

10. Ibid.

11. Ibid.

12. Elie Wiesel, *A Beggar in Jerusalem* (New York: Random House, 1970), p. 208.

Chapter 8

1. Irving Abrahamson, "Elie Wiesel: Speaking Truth to Power," *Reform Judaism*, Fall 1985, p. 9.

2. Edward B. Fiske, "Elie Wiesel: Archivist With a Mission," *New York Times*, January 31, 1973, p. 64.

3. Ibid.

4. Elie Wiesel, *Against Silence*, ed. Irving Abrahamson (New York: Holocaust Library, 1985), vol. 1., p. 35.

5. Ibid., vol. 3, p. 149.

6. Ibid., pp. 152–155.

7. Henry Kamm, "Marchers With Food Aid Get No Cambodian Response," *New York Times*, February 7, 1980, p. A3.

8. James M. Markham, "Elie Wiesel Gets Nobel Prize for Peace as 'Messenger'," *New York Times*, October 15, 1986, p. A10.

9. Personal interview with Elie Wiesel, November 2, 1992.

10. Ibid.

11. Markham, p. A10.

Chapter 9

1. Personal interview with Elie Wiesel, November 2, 1992.

2. Personal interview with Janet McCord, October 14, 1992.

3. Personal interview with Lyle Linder, November 9, 1992.

4. Personal interview with Elie Wiesel, November 2, 1992.

5. Elie Wiesel class at Boston University, November 2, 1992.

6. Personal interview with Joe Kanofsky, October 14, 1992.

7. Elie Wiesel class at Boston University, November 2, 1992.

8. Personal interview with Joe Kanofsky, October 14, 1992.

9. Personal interview with Janet McCord, October 14, 1992.

10. Personal interview with Martha Hauptman, October 14, 1992.

11. Ibid.

12. Personal interview with Elane Norych Geller, October 15, 1992.

13. Jonathan Dorfman, "The Paradox of Elie Wiesel," *Boston Globe*, March 13, 1991, p. 79.

14. Ibid.

15. Elie Wiesel, "A Mideast Peace: Is It Impossible?" *New York Times*, June 23, 1988, p. A23.

16. Personal interview with Joe Kanofsky, October 14, 1992.

17. Personal interview with Elie Wiesel, November 2, 1992.

18. Ibid.

19. Ibid.

20. Elizabeth Devereaux, "Elie Wiesel," *Publisher's Weekly*, April 6, 1992, p. 39.

21. "Wiesel's Speech at Nobel Ceremony," *New York Times*, December 11, 1986, p. A12.

22. Michael Kimmelman, "Making Art of the Holocaust: New Museum, New Works," *New York Times*, April 23, 1993, p. A24.

23. Ibid.

Further Reading

Books

Adler, David A. *We Do Remember the Holocaust.* New York: Henry Holt, 1989.

Altshuler, David A. *Hitler's War Against the Jews.* New York: Behrman House, 1978.

Chiankin, Miriam. *A Nightmare in History.* New York: Clarion Books, 1987.

Cohen, Barbara. *Tell Us Your Secret.* New York: Bantam, 1989. (Holocaust fiction)

Landau, Elaine. *Nazi War Criminals.* New York: Franklin Watts, 1990.

Ossawski, Leonie. *Star Without a Sky.* Minneapolis: Lerner Publications, 1985. (Holocaust fiction)

Rabinowitz, Dorothy. *About the Holocaust.* New York: American Jewish Committee, 1979.

Rhue, Morton. *The Wave.* New York: Dell, 1981. (Holocaust fiction)

Schoenberner, Gerhard. *The Yellow Star.* New York: Bantam, 1973.

Wiesel, Elie. *Night.* New York: Hill and Wang, 1960.

Zisenwine, David W. *Anti-Semitism in Europe: Sources of the Holocaust.* New York: Behrman House, 1976.

Videos

Anne Frank in Maine (a junior high school class in Maine performs *The Diary of Anne Frank* and studies the Holocaust), 28 minutes. Anti-Defamation League of B'nai Brith, 823 United Nations Plaza, New York, NY 10017.

The Camera of My Family (the story of one upper-middle-class German Jewish family before and during Nazi years), 20 minutes. Anti-Defamation League.

The Holocaust: A Teenager's Experience (the story of a 12-year-old boy's harrowing experience in Nazi death camps, some graphic footage), 30 minutes. United Learning, 6633 West Howard Street, Niles, IL 60648.

The Klan: A Legacy of Hate in America (documentary narrated by actor James Whitmore, devoted mostly to KKK activities over last 30 years, racist content), 30 minutes. Films, Inc., 5547 North Ravenswood Avenue, Chicago, IL 60640.

More Than Broken Glass: Memories of Kristallnacht (news footage, photographs, and interviews with witnesses tell story of Kristallnacht), 31 minutes. Ergo Media, P.O. Box 2037, Teaneck, NJ 07666.

Through Our Eyes (true stories of children caught up in Holocaust), 27 minutes. IBT Publishing, Inc., 3747 West Granville, Chicago, IL 60659.

To Know Where They Are (a father and daughter travel to Poland to search for traces of lost ancestors), 28 minutes. Anti-Defamation League.

Tomorrow Came Much Later (high school students travel with Holocaust survivor to Nazi death camps), 58 minutes. Coronet Film and Video, 420 Academy Drive, Northbrook, IL 60062.

Weapons of the Spirit, classroom version (moving remembrance of courageous French civilians who saved Jews of one village from death by Nazis), 38 minutes. Anti-Defamation League.

Index

125

About The Author

Michael A. Schuman has written on numerous subjects, ranging from travel to sports to history. His byline has appeared in several magazines and over ninety newspapers including *The Boston Globe, The New York Daily News, The Chicago Tribune, The Miami Herald, The San Francisco Examiner* and *The Los Angeles Times.* He has written five travel books and is an avid traveler, having visited fourteen countries and all forty-eight contiguous states in the U.S. Mr. Schuman lives in New Hampshire with his wife, Patri, and daughters, Trisha and Alexandra.